THE DEE W

From Prestatyn or Hoylake through Chester and Llangollen to the source

David Berry

KITTIWAKE

About the author

David is an experienced walker, with an interest in local history. He is the author of a series of Kittiwake walks guidebooks covering North Wales, where he lives, as well as a freelance writer for Walking Wales magazine. Whether on a riverside ramble or mountain walk he greatly appreciates the beauty, culture and history of the landscape and hopes that his comprehensive guidebooks will encourage people to explore on foot its diverse scenery and rich heritage. He has undertaken many long distance walks, including coast-to-coast crossings of England, Scotland and Wales.

He has worked as a Rights of Way surveyor across North Wales and served as a member of Denbighshire Local Access Forum.

Thanks

I wish to express my appreciation for the helpful advice and information I have received from a wide range of individuals and organisations, too numerous to mention, that I have consulted during the course of this project. I would particularly like to thank staff in local authority Highways Departments, and the Snowdonia National Park Authority for their practical support in upgrading key sections of the route. Also Flintshire Countryside Service for its assistance on the coastal section.

David Berry
www.davidberrywalks.co.uk

Published by Kittiwake
3 Glantwymyn Village Workshops, Glantwymyn, Machynlleth,
Montgomeryshire SY20 8LY
© Text, map research & photographs: David Berry 2009.
Minor revisions 2011.
© Maps: Kittiwake 2009.
Care has been taken to be accurate.
However neither the author nor the publisher can accept responsibility for any errors which may appear, or their consequences. If you are in any doubt about access, check before you proceed. See page 118.

Printed by MWL, Pontypool.

ISBN: 978 1 902302 66 9

Contents

Introduction

The Route

Guidance Notes and Useful Information

The river near Carrog

INTRODUCTION

The concept and trail development

The **River Dee, or Afon Dyfrdwy** as it is known in Wales, is one of the most historic and beautiful rivers in Britain, passing through a changing landscape of high scenic quality. Starting life in the mountains south west of Llanuwchllyn in the southern area of Snowdonia National Park, the river flows through Llyn Tegid, the largest natural lake in Wales, containing among other fish the unique gwyniad. It continues along the broad wooded valley to Corwen, then heads eastwards through the stunningly beautiful steep-sided valley past Llangollen, before meandering in timeless fashion northwards through the borderland flood plains to its tidal limit at Chester weir. From here it flows along a long tidal estuary, with its mudflats, saltmarshes, sand dunes and low cliffs, which for centuries was an important shipping route and is now internationally renowned for its birdlife habitats.

The Dee passes through many attractive historic towns and villages, from the Welsh-speaking communities of Y Bala and Llanuwchllyn to the former ports and industrial villages that developed along both sides of the Dee Estuary, which separates North Wales from England. En route it passes the historic market towns of Corwen and Llangollen, the attractive border communities of Chirk, Overton, Bangor-on-Dee, Holt and Farndon, and the historic Roman city of Chester, one of the most beautiful cities in Britain, which for centuries was the principal port at the head of the estuary. It passes many places of interest – castles, old churches, ancient bridges, splendid examples of canal and railway engineering, plus much more.

With such a wealth of delightful scenery, heritage and interest, it had seemed to me for a number of years that the river Dee had great potential as a long distance regional cross-border walking trail, similar in concept to the Wye Valley Walk, which I had enjoyed immensely. In July 2003 I finally had the opportunity of exploring this possibility when I began a feasibility study of such a trail as a voluntary project under the *You and Your Community Millennium Awards Scheme*, managed by the Wales Council for Voluntary Action.

The feasibility study involved detailed surveying of potential route sections and identifying available public transport and facilities that would support the trail. It also involved consultation with local authorities and statutory agencies, including the Dee Partnership Group, regarding the concept, route options, and infrastructure/maintenance problems.

The study was very time-consuming, but at the end of the 8 months project I was able to present a feasibility study report to relevant bodies. My main conclusion was that the concept of a long distance trail following the river from the mouth of the Dee estuary to its source in southern Snowdonia was viable, and had considerable potential recreational and economic value. It met key objectives in the long term *Walking Tourism Strategy for Wales* adopted by the Wales Tourist Board and Countryside Council for Wales in 2003.

Its findings were well received:

'Your proposal sounds fantastic!' (*Welsh Development Agency*); 'The concept has merits and would benefit North Wales and local communities' (*Wrexham County Borough*); 'We consider that your proposal has the potential to be very attractive to walkers' (*Cheshire County Council*); 'We would certainly be in favour of such a project' (*Flintshire County Council*); 'I am very supportive of the initiative you have taken with regard to the Dee Way, which I feel is a very worthwhile project' (*Countryside Council for Wales*). The concept was also supported by other bodies including *Snowdonia National Park Authority*, *North Wales Ramblers Association* and *Denbighshire Local Access Forum*.

However, in spite of the wide positive response from local authorities and key statutory agencies, it became increasingly apparent that the formal collaborative cross-border, inter-authority willingness and effort required to develop the trail would be unlikely. Instead some local authorities continued to develop their own local small-scale walking initiatives near the Dee.

Therefore I decided to continue working independently to progress the concept, liaising with individual agencies and monitoring progress on local developments. My aim was to enable people to enjoy the delightful new walking opportunities along the Dee at the earliest opportunity.

I was particularly encouraged by the commitment given by relevant Highways authorities to undertake identified footpath improvement work. In Wrexham County Borough, for instance, an early and constructive response by the authority to blocked paths has resulted in an extensive and little known section of the Dee being opened up between Holt and Bangor-on-Dee.

Gradually the trail has evolved with further key developments taking place to improve the Dee Way route:

– the completion of Denbighshire County Council's Dee Valley Way, on which I advised.

– the upgrading of a riverside off-road cycle/walkway between Connah's Quay and the Old Port, Chester, where it links with a new riverside walkway created by Chester City Council.

– the adoption and upgrading by Snowdonia National Park Authority of my route from Y Bala as the northern section of a planned waymarked trail around Llyn Tegid.

– the completion in late 2008 of new pedestrian road crossings following the major upgrading of the A550 and A5117 trunk roads which had breached the route between Shotwick and Saughall.

– the development by Flintshire County Council's Coastal Unit of a new section of the planned Dee Coastal Path between Greenfield and Flint, providing for the first time a continuous route for walkers along this area of the estuary. This is part of the Welsh Assembly Government's initiative to create a continuous footpath around the coast of Wales scheduled for completion in 2012.

– the planned installation of new footbridges in early 2009 by Wrexham County Borough to gain secure access to my original preferred route to avoid a section of road walking on the Cheshire/Wrexham border.

Throughout this time I have periodically resurveyed the route, regularly checking path improvements and local developments on the ground.

The Dee Way

The trail that I have devised offers:

– a continuous **long distance trail** of up to 142 miles from Prestatyn, and up to 132 miles from Hoylake, to the river's source, with a choice of routes on some sections. (The final 6 mile section to the source and back, across open upland country, is optional.)

– alternative routes along both the Welsh and English sides of the Dee Estuary to Chester, which can easily be combined to make an excellent 57½ mile **Dee Estuary walk**.

– opportunities for **multi-day walks** and **day/half-day** walks of variable lengths. A key feature of the trail is that it is supported by easily accessible public transport throughout its length, allowing each section to be undertaken as linear day walks. I have broken the trail down into **23 linear walks** linked to local transport, with other longer combinations suggested.

– an exhilarating 14 mile **upland circuit of Llyn Tegid**.

– a fascinating insight into the history of the the river from Roman times, including its maritime and industrial past, and border battles, as well as the history and culture of the many diverse communities that the trail passes through.

The direction of the trail following the river upstream is similar to other well-established river trails, enabling long distance walkers to build up their fitness and stamina for the more demanding later hill sections. The trail follows public rights of way, permissive paths and open access land near the source, using a combination of paths, bridleways, tracks, former railway lines, canal towpaths, designated cycle/walkways, as it passes through a diverse landscape and range of communities

The trail crosses the border between England and Wales, through seven local authority areas – the Metropolitan Borough of Wirral, the new Cheshire West and Chester, Flintshire County Council, Wrexham Borough Council, Denbighshire County Council, Gwynedd Council, and briefly Shropshire County Council.

The trail links with other national and promoted recreational routes – Offa's Dyke Path, North Wales Path, The Clwydian Way, The Marches Way, The Maelor Way, Wat's Dyke Way, and the proposed North West Coastal Trail.

The start and end of the trail offer good public transport links with the national transport network to facilitate access to the start of the trail and departure home from the finish to anywhere in Britain.

The new flexible and diverse walking opportunities will appeal to local residents, day visitors and tourists, and all ages and abilities. The route will attract experienced walkers who enjoy the challenge of completing a continuous themed walking trail, people who simply seek the tranquility of attractive river, estuary or hill scenery, or those who want to learn more about an area's rich heritage by visiting buildings and diverse places of historical interest as part of a walk.

People with special needs

Certain sections of the Dee Way, which are off-road, flat and have hard surfaces, and are easily accessible by public transport or private vehicle, offer opportunities for less mobile people and those with disabilities, including sensory impairment. These include promenades, the Llangollen Canal towpath, the Wirral Way from West Kirby to Parkgate, and the riverside off-road cycle/walkway from Wepre Riverside car park, Connah's Quay to the Old Port, Chester. Similar opportunities are provided by Chester's new riverside promenade between the Old Port and the Groves.

The River Dee

The Dee is one of the most regulated rivers in Europe in order to manage the extraction of water for drinking, industrial and agricultural use and for meeting the requirements of the Llangollen Canal, control flooding, protect important fisheries and manage recreational activities. The river provides good quality drinking water primarily for Merseyside and Cheshire. During low flow periods, water is released from Llyn Celyn, via Llyn Tegid, and Llyn Brenig reservoirs into the river.

The Dee provides a range of wildlife habitats, including scarce species such as the otter and water vole. The river is famous for its migrating salmon and sea-trout and an important coarse fishing river for other species such as dace, grayling, roach, bream and chub. There is some commercial sea-fishing for fluke, mullet, bass and shrimp, and regulated cockling in the estuary.

The Dee is popular with canoeists, with Llangollen having one of the best white water courses in Britain, holding national and international events. However, as the Dee is a Special Area of Conservation and sections of the river are protected as SSSI's, canoeing is restricted to protect fishing and wildlife. Rowing, sailing and pleasure craft are popular upstream from Chester.

The river serves as the natural boundary between England and Wales along its estuary to south of Holt and for many centuries the Dee valley has been a strategic route into the heartland of North Wales. It has attracted man since prehistoric times and many of its bridges stand on ancient crossing points, used by traders, travellers and marching armies. Some of these have witnessed border conflicts between the Welsh and English, and the Royalists and Parliamentarians during the Civil War.

The Dee Estuary

The Dee estuary, stretching between Flintshire on the North Wales coast and the Wirral peninsula, serves as a natural boundary between England and Wales. It is an internationally renowned and protected Nature Reserve (a RAMSAR site and Site of Special Scientific Interest [SSSI]), its mudflats and saltmarshes providing feeding and resting for thousands of migrating wading birds and wildfowl over winter. It supports over 10% of the wading bird population of Britain and the only breeding colony of little terns in Wales. It is also known for its treacherous tides and constantly shifting sands and has a fascinating maritime and industrial history. The unpredictable navigability of the river led to the rise and fall of various estuary ports during the many centuries that the Dee was an important shipping route.

The Romans realised the river's strategic importance and built their fort Deva (Chester) at the head of what was then a wide arm of the sea. It later developed as a thriving seaport and the administrative centre for shipping in both North Wales and North West England.

Originally, the natural course of the river followed the Cheshire side of the estuary through a series of channels, and silting of the river became an increasing problem, making it difficult for ships reaching Chester by the 15thC. This led to a succession of new ports developing in turn along the Wirral coast.

Eventually, after an Act of Parliament in 1732, a new channel, over 7 miles long, was constructed from below what is now Connah's Quay through the marsh to join the original river course at Chester. It took 4 years to complete and involved digging a trench 80 feet wide and 8 feet deep by hand, with the help of horsepower – a major engineering feat of its day. About 1½ million tons of excavated spoil was used to form the north bank of the channel, which was pitched with stone. In April 1737, the New Cut was opened and remains to the present day.

Its purpose was to revive Chester's fortunes as a port – short lived as it turned out – but it opened up a new chapter in the estuary's history. The canalisation of the river diverted its course to the Welsh side of the estuary, leading to the eventual demise of the principal Wirral port of Parkgate, a thriving passenger port to Ireland, whilst bringing trade and prosperity to Flintshire. Connah's Quay became a major port, principally trading in bricks and tiles from Buckley, and shipbuilding flourished at Queensferry and Saltney. By the mid 19thC the waterfront boasted warehouses and wharves, some of which remain today, serving the industrial activities developing alongside the river.

Over the centuries the estuary has witnessed Roman soldiers passing by on their way to Deva, troops embarking on campaigns by English kings against the Welsh and Irish, magnificent sailing boats of increasing size plying their trade between Chester and Europe, passenger ferry services across the Dee, and in the early 20thC, coastal sailing ships, tugs, barges, and steamers built locally.

Nowadays, the estuary is a more tranquil scene, with a few small fishing boats and numerous birds for company. The only remaining port of any size is Mostyn Docks near the mouth, with commercial shipping throughout the year. Recently, a goods and passenger ferry to Ireland was established here, but the familiar silting problems meant this was short-lived.

Overview of the trail

The English route to Chester

Hilbre Point, lying at the western tip of the Wirral Peninsula some five miles from Point of Ayr on the Welsh coastline opposite, and easily accessed from Hoylake railway station, is a natural starting point for the trail. From here it heads via Red Rocks Marsh Nature Reserve to West Kirby then follows the Wirral Way, the former Hooton–West Kirby railway line, which was opened as Britain's first Country Park in the 1970s, past Thurstaston Visitor's Centre to Gayton. It then follows the old seawall along the edge of Parkgate Marsh and Gayton Sands RSPB Nature Reserve to Parkgate, now deserted by the waters of the Dee.

From Parkgate, the trail continues along the line of the old coastline to Chester passing through the attractive ancient communities of Burton, Puddington, and Shotwick, which lies at the end of an ancient ford across the Dee to North Wales. After visiting the site of 11thC Shotwick Castle, the trail continues to Saughall, and later follows a railway path and canal to Tower Wharf and the nearby Old Port in Chester.

The Welsh route to Chester

Whilst Point of Ayr at the mouth of the estuary is the natural starting point for the Dee Way from North Wales, the trail starts from the end of Offa's Dyke Path on the promenade at Prestatyn, easily accessible from the railway station. It follows the coast via Gronant Dunes and Talacre Warren Nature Reserve to Point of Ayr, with its 19thC lighthouse. From Talacre to Flint the route continues with the Wales Coast Path currently being developed by Flintshire County Council. The trail first passes Point of Ayr Nature Reserve, with an optional visit to a RSPB Hide, then heads to Ffynnongroyw.

Unfortunately the tidal mudflats, railway line and Mostyn Docks militate against a continuing coastal route, so the trail heads inland via delightful ancient woodland, later rejoining the estuary at Mostyn. From Llannerch-y-mor, the trail follows the estuary to Greenfield Dock. It then diverts through Greenfield Valley, now a Heritage Park containing 12thC Basingwerk Abbey and the remains of 18thC mills and factories, to the historic market town Holywell and its famous St Winefride's Holy Well.

Returning to Greenfield Dock the route then follows a new section of the Coastal Path along the edge of the estuary past former ports to the late 13thC Flint Castle. After Connah's Quay it then crosses the river at Hawarden Bridge and continues along the northern bank of the canalised Dee to the Old Port in Chester.

Chester to the source

The Dee Way continues through Chester via a choice of riverside or city walls routes to the Old Dee Bridge, then closely follows the river via the attractive estate villages of Eccleston and Aldford to historic Farndon. From here to Bangor-on-Dee, the trail follows a choice of routes through the flood plain. One follows closely the western side of the river – one of the least known sections of the Dee. The other route takes a higher line to the east of the river, visiting Shocklach and Worthenbury.

The trail then passes through attractive undulating part wooded countryside to Overton and on to the border town of Chirk. It then heads towards the more rugged Dee Valley via the popular Shropshire Union Canal, then a choice of routes to Telford's famous Pontcysyllte aqueduct high above the Dee, now a World Heritage Site. It continues to Llangollen via a scenic up-

Pontcysyllte Aqueduct

land route featuring romantic Castell Dinas Bran, or an easier canalside route.

From Llangollen, famous for its International Eisteddfod, the trail now follows the waymarked Dee Valley Way, a linear waymarked local authority created walk to the historic market town of Corwen. The route meanders through the foothills and attractive side valleys of the Llantisilio Mountain range via Glyndyfrdwy and the delightful riverside village of Carrog, now linked by the Llangollen Steam Railway. From Corwen the trail climbs to the commanding Iron Age hillfort of Caer Drewyn, then follows the river into the Upper Dee Valley to Cynwyd. After a choice of routes to Llandrillo, one via the foothills of the nearby Berwyn mountains, the trail continues via Llandderfel and Llanfor to the historic market town of Y Bala in the Welsh-speaking heartland.

The next section takes you through part of the southern area of Snowdonia National Park to Llanuwchllyn on a choice of routes across the hills and open upland pastures above beautiful Llyn Tegid, the largest natural lake in Wales. The trail continues along the Dyfrdwy Valley, then follows the course of the infant river to the edge of Coed Penaran. From here experienced walkers can follow the river through sections of cleared forest, then across remote upland country to its source at the base of Dduallt, where there is a surprise and a mystery awaiting the intrepid walker!

This comprehensive guidebook contains detailed route descriptions with maps, guidance notes and useful information to enable people of all abilities to explore this beautiful historic river and the diverse and beautiful landscape it journeys through. I am especially grateful to Kittiwake for its willingness to include the Dee Way in its portfolio of walks guidebooks.

Whether you tackle the Dee Way as a continuous long distance trail or simply undertake short sections as day walks – enjoy your walking!

HOYLAKE TO PARKGATE

9¼ miles

1 Hoylake to Thurstaston Visitor Centre

5 miles

Hilbre Point at the mouth of the Dee estuary, offering extensive views to nearby Hilbre Island and the Welsh coast beyond, is easily accessed from Hoylake railway station. From here, the route follows the shoreline through the dunes of Red Rocks Marsh Nature Reserve, and on to Marine Lake at West Kirby – the only recommended access point at low tide to Hilbre Island. It then continues to Cubbins Green – a delightful grass shelf overlooking the beach with excellent estuary views, before following the Wirral Way – a designated recreational route for walkers, cyclists and horseriders on a former railway line – to Thurstaston Visitor Centre, which houses interesting displays/exhibitions.

In the early 19thC Hoylake consisted of a few fishermen's cottages. However, the desire of prosperous Birkenhead and Liverpool businessmen for summer homes, and the arrival of the railway, led to the creation of a small thriving seaside resort and commuting town.

Just off the northern shore was once a deep pool protected by the extensive Hoyle sandbank. For centuries it provided a safe anchorage for ships too large to navigate the Dee and shelter for others en route to Liverpool. It was an important embarkation point for sailings to Ireland. In 1689, 90 ships with 10,000 troops sailed from here. A year later, William III, after staying at Gayton Hall, travelled to Hoylake on a route known since as the 'Kings Gap' to sail to Ireland to lead the army to defeat James II at the Battle of the Boyne. The canalisation of the Dee altered the tidal flow and by the late 19thC, the anchorage had all but disappeared.

■ From Hoylake railway station walk past the Royal Mail office to a roundabout at the end of Station Road. Go along The King's Gap opposite. Turn left along Stanley Road to reach the slipway at Hilbre Point/Red Rocks. (An alternative low tide option is to follow The King's Gap to the northern seashore, then walk west along the shore to the boundary corner by the red sandstone rocks of Hilbre Point. Follow the wall to the slipway.) From the top of the slipway, turn left down to cross rocks and pass through a small dune, then bear left along the vegetated edge of the shore to follow a boardwalk path into Red Rocks Marsh Nature Reserve. (Alternatively follow a path along the foreshore to West Kirby beach). Go past an information board on the birds of the Dee Estuary and along the sandy path. After passing a path on the right, the main path continues between fences, soon boardwalked, through an area of reeds and dunes, then past a small pond. At the end of the boardwalked section the path continues beside a fence then

Red Rocks

Hilbre Point

Stanley Road

A553

1

Hoylake

A540

golf course

2

West Kirby

Marine Lake

Cubbins Green

N

P

0 kilometres   1

0 miles   ½

Wirral Way

golf course

caravan park

P

Thurstaston Visitor Centre

rises to a good viewpoint and continues along the top of the dunes, passing the famous Royal Liverpool Golf Course. After an information board on West Kirby dunes, the path descends to West Kirby beach. Continue along this popular beach to reach South Parade, West Kirby.

West Kirby is one of the oldest settlements on the Wirral, with Viking connections. Like Hoylake, the arrival of the railway in 1867 developed the small fishing and farming community into a prosperous commuting

town and seaside resort. Although overshadowed by Hoylake as a port, it did have a small fleet in the 16thC, but its trade, which included animal skins, steadily declined. It apparently once had a reputation for wrecking and smuggling.

The three tidal islands of Little Eye, Middle Eye and Hilbre at the mouth of the Dee estuary are designated a Local Nature Reserve. Hilbre Island has been occupied since earliest times. Monks from Chester Abbey lived here for nearly 400 years. It has a Telegraph Station built by the Trustees of Liverpool Docks in 1841 as part of a chain stretching from Holyhead on Anglesey to Liverpool. It was used as an embarkation point by both Elizabeth I and Cromwell for their campaigns in Ireland.

2 Walk along the promenade past Wirral Sailing Centre and the Marine Lake. (A popular low tide option is to follow a walkway around the lake edge.) At the end of South Parade, follow the road away from the shore. (An alternative low tide option is to follow the shoreline to take a waymarked stony path angling up onto Cubbins Green). At a junction continue ahead along the right-hand side of Sandy Lane. Shortly turn right along Macdona Drive. At its end, follow the surfaced path to enter Cubbins Green. Walk along this grass shelf – *enjoying panoramic estuary views* – to the last seat, then follow the

15

View across the estuary from Cubbins Green

path away from the estuary to join the Wirral Way. Turn right and follow the wide path to Caldy car park, then its access lane to a road. Continue on the Wirral Way along the former railway line, passing under three bridges to reach the former station platform and nearby Thurstaston Visitor Centre. A short diversion will take you to the cliffs and good views across the estuary.

For over 70 years a single track railway operated between Hooton and West For over 70 years a single track railway operated between Hooton and West Kirby, with links to Birkenhead. At its peak the line *had 12 passenger trains each day in each direction. Early morning trains, carrying commuters to Liverpool, were timed to link with Woodside ferries. Day excursions brought people to the seaside and Parkgate. Freight trains carried coal from Ness Colliery, milk, potatoes, livestock, fish, shrimps and prawns. The station at Thurstaston was situated one mile from the village due to objections from the owner of Dawpool Hall. The line finally closed in 1962 and was then opened in 1973 as Wirral Country Park – the first in Britain. Just offshore from Thurstaston was a deep water anchorage known as Dawpool/Redbank, which was in use between the 14th and 19thC.*

2 Thurstaston Visitor Centre to Parkgate

4¼ miles

Thurstaston Visitor Centre ❶

cliffs

Wirral Way

Heswall Fields

Heswall

Gayton ❷

P

Parkgate

PO school

N

The route continues with the Wirral Way for just over 2½ miles to Gayton, then follows the old seawall along the edge of Parkgate Marsh and Gayton Sands RSPB Nature Reserve to Parkgate, once a thriving passenger port for Ireland and a fashionable bathing resort, now deserted by the waters of the Dee.

Continue with the Wirral Way, past an optional National Trust circuit of Heswall Fields and cliffs, later passing under Farr Hall Drive Bridge to reach the bend of a road after two miles. Continue along Davenport Road/Riverbank Road. Just past Riverbank Close, on the bend, rejoin the Wirral Way. Continue along the old railway cutting. Just before a bridge, follow a path on the left up to the road. Turn right and follow the road down to its end at Gayton Cottage by the edge of the expansive area of marsh.

It is hard to imagine that this was once the high water mark of the Dee, providing an anchorage for ships in the Middle Ages, and used as a crossing point by Edward I in 1277 to Flint after a stay at Shotwick Castle. In the early 19thC a regular sailing boat ferry service operated between here and Greenfield on the Welsh coast. Gayton Cottage, the former ferry house, could accommodate up to 20 travellers.

The retreat of the tidal waters has left a vast area of mudflats, sandflats and saltmarsh that now form Parkgate Marsh and Gayton Sands RSPB Nature Reserve. These habitats provide rich feeding and safe roosting areas for one of the largest wintering areas of ducks and wading birds in the British Isles.

0 kilometres 1

0 miles ½

17

Parkgate

2 Follow the path along the top of the red sandstone former sea-wall. You can just about see the water of the Dee beneath the Welsh hills opposite. Soon Parkgate is visible ahead. After a kissing gate, continue past The Old Baths car park and along its access lane to reach the road by The Boathouse.

At the beginning of the 18thC, an anchorage known as the Beer House Hole had developed just offshore from the previous inn on this site. As Parkgate emerged as a premier passenger terminal for Ireland, a popular ferry also operated across the Dee to Flint. At first it carried only passengers, but by the late 18thC also horses and other animals. Later a landing-stage was built at the Ferry House Inn, as it was then known, to remove the indignity of ladies being carried into the boats! The ferry ceased about 1860. A short-lived steam packet service to Bagillt began in 1817.

Continue by the old sea-wall through Parkgate along The Parade, built as a promenade in the 1840s for visitors.

The attractive, largely 18thC, frontage of Parkgate is a reminder of its former prestigious past. It began as a village on land previously used as a deer park, then in the 18thC became a major passenger port for Ireland and a fashionable seaside resort. Ships anchored in the main channel of the river, originally 50 yards from the seawall.

Famous travellers included the composer Handel, for the first performance of 'The Messiah' in Dublin in 1741, and John Wesley, the preacher, who made numerous crossings. Turner painted here, and visitors included Mrs Fitzherbert, who subsequently married the Prince of Wales, later George IV, and Emma Hart of nearby Ness, later Lady Hamilton, mistress of Admiral Lord Nelson.

By 1815, the Dee no longer flowed along the Wirral shore, ending the Parkgate-Dublin service. Parkgate then became a fishing village famous for its shrimps, and a well-known bathing resort until the 1930s, when the water reached the seawall only on exceptionally high tides. It remains popular with visitors today.

PARKGATE TO THE OLD PORT, CHESTER

14½ miles

3 Parkgate to Puddington

5 miles

This section follows the edge of the marsh along the line of the old coastline, passing the important former anchorage sites of Old Quay and Denhall, and visiting the attractive ancient villages of Burton, once a thriving port, and Puddington.

1 At the far end of Parkgate, when the road bends left near the Old Quay pub, keep on alongside the sea-wall to its end by Far End cottage. Follow a path along the top of sandstone blocks and on to reach a lane by Riverside. Turn right along the lane. At its end, go along an enclosed path, then continue along Manorial Road South. On the bend, turn right on a signposted path (Old Quay ½ mile) to reach the edge of the marsh. Turn left to follow the path along its edge. After a stile the path continues along the edge of a field, through a gap in the hedge boundary corner, and on to cross a stream – with the remains of the old sea-wall to your right. Continue to cross a sandstone stile at Old Quay.

It the 1540s a stone pier was built here, some 10 miles down river from Chester, to serve as its 'out port', when navigation to the city by large ships was becoming difficult. From an anchorage nearby, goods were landed on the quay and taken by small boats to Chester. It was known as 'New Key' and was in regular use until early 18thC, when it was replaced by the new port at Parkgate. After its decline it became known as 'Old Quay'. Adjoining the quay was Key House, a prominent landmark and at one time a prison.

Continue along the marsh edge, then follow a track to a road end at Little Neston. *You pass the site of the former Little Neston Colliery. For almost 180 years, until its closure in 1928, coal was extracted from seams running two miles under the estuary. For many years it was transported along underground canals in small boats, by boatmen pushing against the roof.*

2 Keep ahead along the rough lane to reach Harp Inn. *It was built for miners, many of whom came from Staffordshire, and is now popular with wildfowlers returning from shooting on the marshes.* Continue along the lane. *After about 100 yards, just to your right are the large red sandstone blocks of Denhall Quay. It was a popular anchorage during the 15thC and 16thC, and was still in use at the end of the 17thC when 10 ships and 55 men were registered here. Unlike the Old Quay, it remained navigable after the New Cut in 1737, and was used to ship coal from the nearby colliery to Ireland during the 18th and 19thC* *until silting finally prevented barges reaching the quay.*

Continue along the lane through a small residential area, then follow a path along the edge of the expansive marsh. *It contains both a military firing range and a wildfowl reserve established in 1964 by the Dee Wildfowlers and Wetlands Management Club, who are licensed to shoot wildfowl such as duck and wigeon.* Follow a lane past Denhall House Farm, then Marsh Cottage to a road. Keep ahead and follow the road as it rises away from the estuary and crosses the railway to eventually reach a junction at the outskirts of Burton.

3 Here turn sharp left up the road (or right into Burton). After about 150 yards, take a signposted path through a kissing gate up on the right. Go up the path, soon bearing right into Burton Wood. After a few yards, the path rises left up through the trees to a signposted cross-path leading from a nearby stone stile. Follow it right through the wood, soon near a wooden fence. At a crossroad of paths by a finger post, turn right down steps past Rake Cottage. *(About 200 yards further ahead on the path are 17thC Quakers' Graves. Denied burial in a consecrated graveyard, they were said to have been buried in a standing-up position.)* Continue down the stony track to the road by thatched Barn End, formerly the Fisherman's Arms. Follow the road through the village.

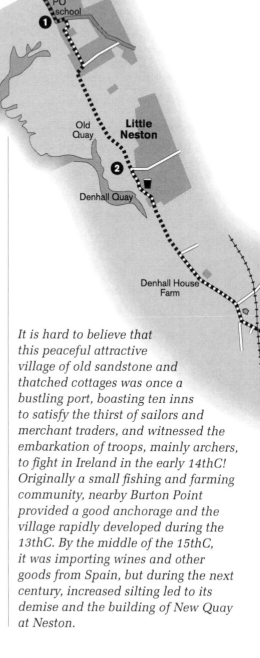

It is hard to believe that this peaceful attractive village of old sandstone and thatched cottages was once a bustling port, boasting ten inns to satisfy the thirst of sailors and merchant traders, and witnessed the embarkation of troops, mainly archers, to fight in Ireland in the early 14thC! Originally a small fishing and farming community, nearby Burton Point provided a good anchorage and the village rapidly developed during the 13thC. By the middle of the 15thC, it was importing wines and other goods from Spain, but during the next century, increased silting led to its demise and the building of New Quay at Neston.

4 Shortly turn right along Puddington Lane, past Bishop Wilson school and on towards Puddington. As the road bends left, go along the track ahead past Old Hall Nurseries and the entrance to The Stables to a kissing gate. Keep ahead past barns to another kissing gate and on to follow a driveway to a junction in the centre of Puddington. Follow a signposted path past the side of the house opposite. Shortly, turn left along an access lane past dwellings to the road.

Denhall Quay

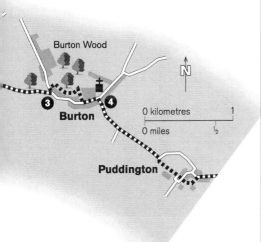

This quiet hamlet, mentioned in the Doomsday Book, was for centuries the seat of the Massey family, who lived at Old Puddington Hall, built in 1490. Its members fought in many famous battles both in Britain and Europe, and two were knighted for their efforts. William Massey, the last of the direct line, fought against the Royalists at Preston in 1715. Faced with defeat, he rode non stop, forded the Mersey and crossed the Wirral. On reaching the hall, the exhausted horse dropped dead. Their efforts were in vain, for shortly afterwards, William was imprisoned in Chester Castle, where he died the following year.

21

4 Puddington to Saughall

4½ miles

This section follows mainly field paths to the ancient village of Shotwick, once an important port and crossing point of the Dee. After negotiating the A550 and the A5117 by new crossings following major roadworks recently completed, it later follows upgraded permissive paths past the site of Shotwick Castle and through Dingle Wood to Saughall.

I At the road turn right to leave the village. On the bend, turn right along Chapel House Lane on a path signposted to Shotwick, past houses. At minor crossroads keep ahead. Go past the lane angling to Home Farm Stables, then take the next right fork. Shortly turn left on a signposted path along a green track opposite the stables. At the field corner, angle right across the next field and on past the end of a lily pool. Follow the waymarked path to the tree boundary ahead, then follow it right to go through two small gates in the field corner. Follow the boundary on your right through two fields to go through another small gate. Follow the narrow hedge-lined path to join a green track which takes you past farm buildings, then the front of Shotwick Hall. *It was built in the 1660s as a replacement for a nearby ancient manor-house by Joseph Hockenhull, whose family had held the manor from the reign of Edward I.* Follow its access lane to Shotwick village. At the junction, a short diversion right takes you past attractive cottages to the delightful red sandstone St Michael's Church. Return to the junction.

Shotwick lies at the end of an ancient ford across the Dee to North Wales. It was an important trading route since before Norman times, and by the Middle Ages a well- established 'Saltesway' for the carrying of Cheshire salt. Despite the hazards of shifting sands, this tidal crossing was for many travellers preferable to other longer land journeys prone to highwaymen. Several armies crossed the ford, in 1245 under Henry III and in 1278 and 1284 under Edward I, in campaigns against the Welsh. The ford was in use until the 18thC. 14thC records indicate a ferryboat also operated here.

For a period during the 15th/16thC, when large ships were unable to reach Chester, Shotwick was the main Dee port, providing a deep tidal anchorage for ships to offload their cargoes. At that time the tidal waters lapped the churchyard walls of St Michael's, which dates from the 12thC. The porch stonework has deep groves made by archers sharpening their arrows. The village buildings are mainly 17thC and include the former Greyhound Inn.

2 Follow the road out of the village, then go through a kissing gate set back up on the right. Go down the field, and across a gated footbridge, then go up the edge of the next field to go through a kissing gate. Turn right through a nearby small gate, then head left across the field to a kissing gate and on to the A550. Turn right then cross the road by the Pegasus traffic light controlled crossing and follow a pathway/cycleway to reach Woodbank Lane. Continue NE. along this minor road past Grange Farm, then

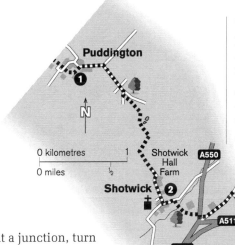

the edge of two fields, then turns left past the earthworks of Shotwick castle. *It was built in the 11thC above the Dee to defend the nearby major crossing point of the river, used by English Kings during the 12th and 13thC as a base for campaigns in Wales and Ireland, after which it gradually fell into ruin.* After a kissing gate the path crosses a stream and continues through Dingle Wood to cross a footbridge. Soon it descends to another footbridge, then climbs onto an

at a junction, turn right and follow Lodge Lane to cross a bridge over the A5117. Bear right down the access lane towards the farm. At the fence corner turn left along the service track, then at the end of the second field on the left you join the original public footpath severed by the roadworks (signposting requested). Follow the path S.E. along the edge of several fields. After a footbridge continue up the field edge to go through a kissing gate in the hedge corner. Turn right. (An alternative route after crossing the A5117 is to bear left down to a junction, then turn right to continue along Lodge Lane past Shotwick Lodge Farm, with its ancient tithe barn. At the far end of a wood, take a signposted path through a kissing gate on the right. Go along the edge of two fields through further kissing gates to point **3**. Continue ahead.)

3 Here a direct route to Saughall continues SE. as shown. However, the trail continues with the waymarked kissing gated path along

embankment near the wood edge – *the old coastline.* After a few yards, at a path junction turn left, soon emerging from the trees and continuing along the edge of a small wooded valley. Go past a kissing gate and continue beside the fence. *To your right is Shotwick House, a former manor house built in 1872.* After a footbridge over the stream the permissive path passes along the wood edge to a kissing gate into a field. Keep ahead, then turn right across a stiled footbridge. Go over a track and on ahead across the field to pass through a narrow strip of woodland, then follow the field path to a kissing gate to reach

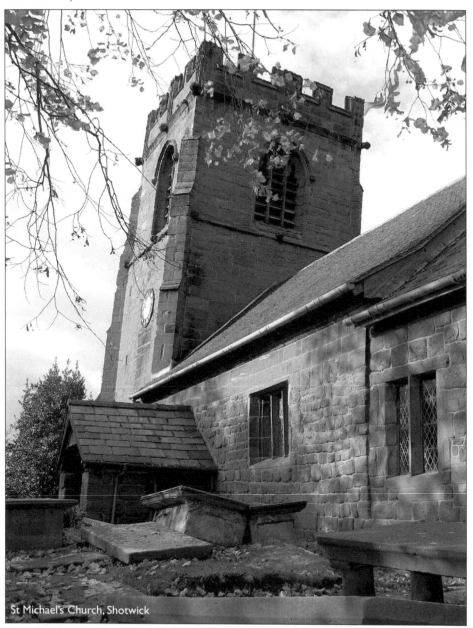

St Michael's Church, Shotwick

the main street in Saughall. (A Post Office/stores is to the left, up the road.) *Prior to the New Cut and the land reclamation schemes of the 18thC,* *Great Saughall stood at the edge of the former Dee coastline, and once had an anchorage for ships.*

5 Saughall to the Old Port, Chester

5 miles

The final section to Chester features field paths, an ancient highway, a designated railway path and a delightful section of canalside walking. An alternative route to the railway path is to follow the main road through and out of the village, passing The Greyhound pub on the way.

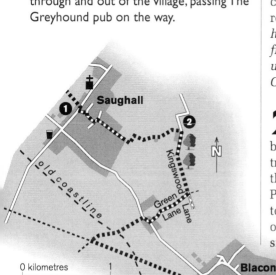

to cross a stile/sleeper bridge in the boundary after 50 yards. Go across the field to go through a kissing gate by a multi-signed finger post. Go across the next field passing to the left of a small pool to another kissing gate and sleeper bridge. Follow the path across the large field towards a house to pass its wooden paddock fence corner, then go along its access track to reach Kingswood Lane. *This ancient highway was part of the 'Saltesway' from Chester to Shotwick Ford and used as a military road to Shotwick Castle.*

2 Turn right along the rough lane, which, after buildings, then becomes a hedge-lined path. At a track junction, turn right to follow the tree-lined track (green lane) to Poplars Farm then its access lane to the road. Cross to the pavement opposite and follow it right to take a signposted path along a tree/hedge lined track. After a stile/gate

1 Turn right and just past Saughall Service Station take a signposted path opposite between houses leading to Smithy Close. At the junction, turn right along Darlington Crescent. At the T-junction turn left, then right along The Ridings. Just after passing Rosewood Grove take a signposted tarmaced path on the left to a kissing gate into a field. Follow the boundary on the right. In the corner turn left

follow the track along the field edge, soon descending the former low cliffs to another stile/gate. The path now angles right through the maize field to

Tower Wharf

its corner, then continues ahead along the next field edge to a stile to join the Chester to Connah's Quay Railway Path – *the former Mickle Trafford freight line is now a narrow linear park and woodland.* Follow the wide cycle/walkway for just over 2 miles east towards Chester, passing through Blacon.

3 After crossing the canal, take the signposted cycleway down to the canal towpath. Turn left and continue along the towpath to eventually reach a small boatyard. Cross the small swing bridge, then bridge 126 across the canal to pass a dry dock. Follow the path between the two canal basins, the larger being Tower Wharf, to where the path splits almost opposite Telford's Warehouse.

Tower Wharf stands at the junction of two canals. The Chester – Nantwich canal, which opened in 1779, was initially a commercial failure, but its extension to Ellesmere Port in 1795 turned Chester into a thriving trading and boat-building centre. Tower Wharf was the HQ of the Shropshire Union

Railways and Canal Company, which owned over 400 narrow boats, flats and barges, most of which were built here. Traditional boat building and repair skills continue to service today's recreational canal traffic.

Between 1795–1840, a popular horse-drawn passenger service operated daily between Tower Wharf and Ellesmere Port, from where passengers transferred to a Mersey packet which sailed to Liverpool in 1801 about 15,000 people a year used this 15,000 people a year used this service.

Here you have a choice of routes through Chester to the Old Dee Bridge: either a riverside route from the Old Port (**A**) or from Tower Wharf via the city walls (**B**). See Section **14**.
To reach the Old Port and the start of route **A** take the path up to a kissing gate at South View road. Cross the road, turn right, then take steps down to the canal. Continue along the canal basin, past a lift bridge and on past a lock to the road. Cross with care to the Dee Lock opposite, where the canal joins the river.

PRESTATYN TO HOLYWELL

15¼ miles

6 Prestatyn to Point of Ayr, Talacre

4¾ miles

The start of the trail from the modern sculpture on the promenade by the Nova Centre in Prestatyn is easily accessed from the town centre railway station. This initial section of the Dee Way follows part of the new Wales Coast Path currently being developed, featuring fine beach and dune scenery, and a prominent 19thC lighthouse at the mouth of the estuary. When passing through at high tide please avoid disturbance to any roosting birds.

The dunes between Prestatyn and Talacre form part of the Gronant Dunes and Talacre Warren SSSI. They are the remnants of a dune system which once stretched along most of the North Wales coastline, and still serve as an important sea defence. The dunes and foreshore are rich in plant, animal, bird and insect life. Plants include the dominant marram grass, and less common species such as sea-holly, pyramidal orchid, sea and portland spurge. The rare natter-jack toad has recently been reintroduced. The foreshore and shingle attract a variety of birds, including wintering waders, cormorants and the only breeding colony of little terns in Wales. The land behind the dune systems was reclaimed from marshland between 1790–1854.

1 From Prestatyn Railway station join the road on its northern side and follow it to traffic lights at the nearby A458. Go along Bastion Road opposite signposted to the Nova Centre/Beaches. On the bend by the Nova Centre go up a pathway ahead past the Cafe Cymru/Information Centre and round to the large Sun sculpture beyond – Dechrau a diwedd (beginning and end) – marking the start/finish of the Offa's Dyke Path. *Here are extensive coastal views west to the Great Orme and the northern mountains of Snowdonia. Directly out to sea is North Hoyle windfarm – the first major offshore one in the U.K., built in 2003. Other later windfarms can be seen.* Walk east along the promenade to its end alongside Barkby Beach car park. Go up the slipway, then follow the signposted Wales Coast Path along a further short section of promenade then a rough path by Gronant Dunes, a designated Local Nature Reserve.

2 Take the next but one signposted path up a wooden walkway, then follow the waymarked Wales Coast Path along the top of the dunes and past the fence corner. At the next waymarker post turn left, then follow the path along the edge of the dunes, past another waymarker post and on through the middle of the expansive dunes, later becoming more enclosed.

A white house visible on the hills above Gronant is the former Voelnant Telegraph station, dating from 1841. It was one of a chain of twelve semaphore stations established between Holyhead and Liverpool to give merchants and shipowners in

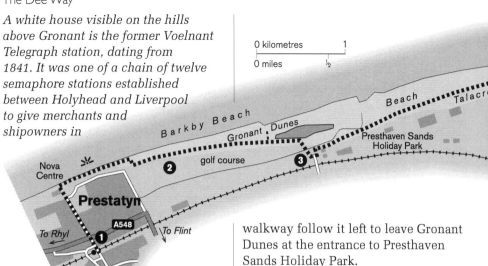

Liverpool early news of the arrival of their ships. Signallers used a powerful telescope to constantly watch the next station in line. They became very skilled and able to relay signals at high speed. Unfortunately, they could not work at night or during bad weather, so about 1860 a new system of electrical transmission between five main stations was gradually introduced.

After ¾ mile you reach a finger post by an information board on the little tern, and a path leading to a viewing platform overlooking Gronant Beach. Follow the path ahead signposted to Presthaven to pass along the southern edge of a small shallow lake (dry sometimes). Shortly, turn right on the signposted path and follow the embanked path inland, soon crossing an inlet known as Prestatyn Gutter. *Shallow draught boats called 'flats' used to travel up this tributary to the outskirts of Prestatyn.* At a wide cycle/walkway follow it left to leave Gronant Dunes at the entrance to Presthaven Sands Holiday Park.

3 Turn left to go through the nearby bridle gate. The path soon bears right alongside Prestatyn Gutter and goes along the top of the dunes to join the end of a wooden walkway. You are now in Gronant Dunes and Talacre Warren SSSI. Follow the stony path to an information board about the natterjack toad. Just beyond take the left fork and follow the waymarked path between dunes and a large wet reedy area. Later continue along the pebbly, then sandy foreshore beneath the large dunes, passing signposted paths into Presthaven Sands. *Low tide reveals a vast expanse of sand and ahead is Point of Ayr lighthouse. It was built in 1819 to replace the original one established here in 1777. Ninety feet high, it had four floors and a blinking light with a range of 19 miles. It has survived a replacement 1844 iron tower, and a later tower built in 1891. Its subsequent uses have included a store, wartime lookout, and holiday home. Point of Ayr also had a lifeboat*

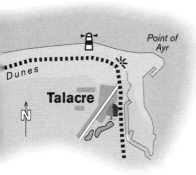

tide.) Go past the lighthouse – there is soft sand around it, so beware – and at a large finger post follow the signed path/bridleway into the dunes. Bear left down to a waymarker post then follow the permissive bridleway east alongside the fence. Shortly take a path up to a viewing platform on the dunes. *Here you have your first view of the tidal river Dee flowing between the Welsh coast and the Wirral.* Go past a large information board and follow the embanked path to reach the road end at Talacre.

station from the early 19thC until the 1920s.

As you near the lighthouse you pass a large post indicating a permissive bridleway leading into the dunes. (This links with a waymarked path through the dunes – an option at high

Talacre had a harbour during the 18th and 19thC, which was later taken over and used by Point of Ayr Colliery which operated until the late 20thC.

Overlooking Barkby Beach

7 Talacre to Mostyn

5½ miles

From Talacre the route goes along a small tidal inlet adjoining Point of Ayr Nature Reserve, an important roosting site for wetland birds, with an optional visit to a RSPB Hide. It continues around the site of the former Point of Ayr colliery and across the Cob into Ffynnongroyw. The tidal mudflats, railway line and Mostyn Docks militate against a continuing coastal route, so the trail loops inland. After passing the former 18thC Garth Mill, it rises through delightful ancient woodland, skirts the Mostyn Estate featuring an unusual lodge, before following a bridleway down to the 17thC Lletty Inn at Mostyn.

1 Just beyond the Talacre Beach information board take the path signposted to Ffynnongroyw. Follow the path along the embankment, later passing the perimeter of BHP gas terminal – *which processes gas piped from platforms visible in Liverpool Bay.* Just before the main path bends left to the large RSPB hide – *a worthwhile diversion* – keep ahead with the waymarked path briefly through trees, then continue along the edge of the former Point of Ayr colliery site. At the boundary corner turn right and follow the signposted path along the wide road. After a while, turn left on a signposted path along another former road to cross a large footbridge over the former colliery railway. Follow the enclosed path near the main coast railway line to eventually reach a lane by a power substation. Turn right to pass under the railway bridge, then go through a kissing gate on the left, signposted to Ffynnongroyw, and another ahead. Now continue along the top of a wide embankment – *known locally as 'The Cob'* – to a kissing gate to reach the A548. Cross the dual carriageway with care to another kissing gate opposite, then follow the path to a road. Turn left into Ffynnongroyw and cross to the pavement opposite.

Ffynnongroyw, meaning 'the clear well' was once an area of tidal mudflats. In 1847, the building of the Chester-Holyhead railway, with its associated embankments prevented the tides from flooding this area. This permitted the construction of the coast road and rows of terraced houses for the colliers of Mostyn and later point of Ayr.

2 Just beyond the Post Office/shop turn right on the signposted path along Well Lane. *This was the original road along the coast.* At its end follow the path beneath woodland to reach the Well. *It has supplied water to the village for generations and was believed to possess healing powers for minor ailments. Women would do their washing in the outflow from the well, and miners would collect water on their way to the pit and reputedly bathe their feet in the outflow on their return. Community standpipes arrived in the 1930s, but the well continued to be used until the 1980s.* Continue along the path then track past the rear of houses to a road (Llinegr Hill). Angle left across the road, then go along Garth Lane. At its end cross the footbridge adjoining the ford and go

Talacre

Gas terminal

hide

1

0 kilometres   1

0 miles   ½

N

Ffynnongroyw

2 well

3 Garth Mill

Nant Felin Blwm

A548

Mostyn

Rhewl-Mostyn

Drybridge Lodge

4

Lletty Inn

has a surprising industrial past. Its Welsh name means 'lead mill', in reference to the ancient lead smelting hearths that once operated in the locality. In addition, shallow coal pits were worked in the valley during the 18th and 19th centuries. The path rises steadily through the wood to eventually leave it by a gate. Turn right along a farm track to a stile/ gate. Continue ahead to follow a low embankment to another stile/ gate. Go half-left to join the boundary ahead, then follow it to cross a stile in the first field

across the front of Garth Mill. *Now an inn, it was built as a water-powered corn mill in 1743, and operated until 1956. It once ground fodder for the pit ponies that worked underground at the nearby Point of Ayr colliery.*

3 Turn left past its gable end then follow a path passing behind the mill and rising up through the trees, soon bearing right. Keep with the main path as it contours across the steeply wooded slopes above the river, the leat which supplied water to power the mill, and the silted-up remains of the former mill-pond in the valley bottom. *This delightful ancient semi-natural woodland of Felin Blwm,*

corner. Go through trees to a nearby road. Follow it left past the entrance to Mostyn Hall to go under Drybridge Lodge. *Built in 1849 this two-storeyed castellated lodge not only has the public road passing underneath it, but also the former horse and carriage drive from Mostyn Hall to Whitford passing through it.*

31

Point of Ayr Nature Reserve

4 At the junction, at the outskirts of Rhewl-Mostyn, turn right, signposted to Maes Pennant. Continue along the road and at the end of the wood take a signposted bridleway on the left. Follow it down into the narrow wooded valley, then turn left to cross a nearby large footbridge over the stream. Follow the bridleway up to leave the wood by a bridle-gate. Go past a cottage – *with a good view across the estuary* – and follow its access track down past houses to a junction. Continue along the rough lane ahead past bungalows, then follow a hedge/tree-lined bridleway down to the car park of the Lletty Inn. *Dating from 1699, the inn has seen life as a warehouse, distillery and smuggler's haven. Note the strange stone carving and description 'the honest man 1699' above the door, whose origins are uncertain.*

8 Mostyn to Greenfield

3½ miles

The trail continues along the edge of the estuary, then visits the small community of Llannerch-y-mor, with its 17thC thatched inn and Abakhan Fabrics Craft & Mill Shop, both offering refreshment options. It then follows a path near the estuary to historic Greenfield Dock and continues to nearby Greenfield.

Mostyn

Lletty Inn

■ Cross the
road with care
then walk along the
pavement. Just past a
house take a signposted
path to cross a footbridge over the
railway line, and on through the trees
to reach a viewing area overlooking
the estuary, with a good view across to
Mostyn Dock.

Mostyn Dock, with its surviving 18thC quay, is the only active large estuary port. During the 19thC, its importance grew with the development of a major local colliery, and the establishment of Mostyn iron-works on reclaimed land. Iron-ore was transported on flat-bottomed boats from ships anchored in mid-river, and the resultant pig iron was shipped to Liverpool. At the beginning of this century, a regular freight/passenger ferry service ran to Ireland, but was short-lived due to

inevitable silting of the channel. More recently, it has been involved in the construction of the nearby windfarms.

Follow the embanked track alongside the edge of the estuary – *a section popular with fishermen* – to the entombed and rusting Duke of Lancaster or 'Fun Ship' – *the sad legacy of a failed private initiative to create an unusual leisure complex on this former ferry, some years ago.* A path continues alongside the dock's perimeter, then follows its access lane under the railway to reach the A548 at Llannerch-y-Mor. Turn left. Please note that the route past the ship has been subject to consultation and possible realignment.

Llanerch-y-mor

Abakhan

0 kilometres 1

0 miles ½

Greenfield
Dock

Greenfield

Basingwerk
Abbey
P

Nearby Abakhan Craft and Mill Shop was converted from an important 18thC lead-smelting works, whose wheelpit and smelting chimney survive. The nearby quay was used by the lead-works.

2 Follow the signposted path along the eastern bank of the

Greenfield Dock

stream to pass back under the low railway bridge. Go along the narrow creek leading to the ship, then bear right along the boulder embanked edge of the estuary to a kissing gate. Continue along the embanked coastal path – *enjoying the seabirds, occasional fishing boats, and views across the ever changing tidal estuary to the Wirral. From the mid-18thC embankments were built to help land to be reclaimed from the salt-marsh, which had originally extended to the coast road between Mostyn and Flint.* After 1½ miles you reach a car park at Greenfield Dock – *with a viewing area and information board overlooking the estuary.*

It is difficult to imagine that this narrow inlet, now used by small boats for shrimp and flounder fishing, was a busy port in the 18th and 19thC. Up to 40 ships once traded from here in raw materials and finished products from industries in the Greenfield Valley. Nothing remains of the large wharf built in the 18thC. In 1802, a sailing ship ferry service between Greenfield-Parkgate-Chester was established. Between 1857–1865, the iron ship 'Fanny' provided a 1½ hour passenger service to Liverpool. In the 1870s two other similar services were shortlived. Shifting channels in the Dee Estuary meant that increasingly only small boats had access to the port, and along with local industries, its importance declined during the 19thC, and by its end, it had also lost its rail link.

From the car park entrance follow nearby Dock Road across the railway line – *noting the elegant former Holywell Junction Station, built 1847-8 and closed in the 1960s* – to reach the A548 in Greenfield. Turn left, then cross the road to the main Greenfield Valley Heritage Park car park.

9 Holywell via the Greenfield Valley

1½ miles

The trail continues through Greenfield Valley, now a Heritage Park, containing various ancient monuments, including the 12thC Basingwerk Abbey, as well as the remains of mills and factories, that made it a major industrial centre in the 18thC. It passes the famous St Winefride's Holy Well, which gave its name to the historic market town of Holywell.

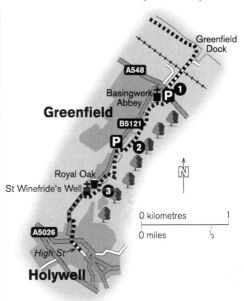

Greenfield Valley, near to sources of lead and other ores, and with easy access by sea to Liverpool, developed rapidly during the 18thC as an important industrial centre, regarded as the cradle of the Industrial Revolution in North Wales. Its constant flow of water – 4,000 gallons a minute which never froze – provided the power for a line of mills and factories that stretched down the narrow valley. It steadily declined during the 19thC with the development of steam power, and the need for larger sites and better port facilities.

1 Head across the car park to an information board and go up the path into the Heritage Park, then follow it around the perimeter of Basingwerk Abbey. *Founded in 1132, it became an important centre for monks of the Cistercian Order until its dissolution by Henry VIII in 1536. They established corn and fulling mills, and created a cultural community, which became the home of many Welsh poets.* After passing the Visitor Centre, with a café nearby, turn left and go

on past the Farm Museum. *Just to the west is a mill pool, all that remains of the important Parys Mine Company copper works, built in 1787 by Thomas Williams, known as 'The Copper King' for his success in producing copper bolts, rudder fittings and sheathing for wooden sailing ships.* A little further on take the lane signposted to various sites, soon passing the site of the former Abbey Wire Mill – *which made copper and brass wire* – and its mill pond. Go past the Lower Cotton Mill – *once an impressive six storey building, powered by an 18 feet high water wheel, used for spinning cotton brought from the Americas between 1785-1840. Later it was used by a miller/flour dealer.*

2 Continue past the large Flour Mill pool, then follow a signed path close to the lake, passing to the right of large iron gates and on through the

35

Basingwerk Abbey

site of Meadow Mill – *which made rollers for printing patterns on cloth and copper sheets.* Now cross over the mill pool dam and on through a car park to its entrance at Bryn Celyn. Go through a kissing gate and follow the path signposted to Greenfield Mills/ Royal Oak, soon passing a former brick clock tower. Just beyond, take the left fork, then after 40 yards bear left to pass around the edge of the remains of Greenfield Mills. *Established in 1776, the Battery Works produced brass pots and pans, which were sent via Liverpool to Africa and exchanged for slaves.* At a rectangular brick chimney, turn right and cross the dam of Battery Pool, then turn left along its edge, soon taking the path's left fork to go through an iron archway by the car park of the nearby Royal Oak.

3 Turn left and follow a stepped path up through the trees. At its top, turn right along a path, soon alongside a wall and past a chimney and on through a kissing gate. Follow the path down to reach the B5121. Follow it left to the entrance of St

Winefride's Well (*open daily 10.00– 16.00*).

The legend of the miracle-working spring begins in 660 AD, when Winefride, a young girl, rejected the advances of Caradog, a local chieftain. In his anger, he cut off her head. Where it came to rest, a spring of crystal water began to flow from the ground. Miraculously, she was restored to life by her uncle St Beuno, and became a nun. Enclosed in an early 16thC chapel, the famous well chamber, with a bath renowned for its healing properties, has attracted pilgrims for many centuries, including Henry V in 1416 and James II, who visited in 1686 to pray for a son. It was once littered with the crutches of the cured. Continue up the road, then turn left through a gateway passing behind St Winefride's Chapel to St James Church, dating from 1770. Follow the pathway up past its congested hillside graveyard and continue up Well Street. Cross the inner ring road to reach Holywell centre. Go along the High Street.

HOLYWELL TO THE OLD PORT, CHESTER

18½ miles

10 Holywell to Flint Castle, Chester

6½ miles

The trail returns down the Greenfield Valley on the former trackbed of the steepest conventional passenger railway in Great Britain. It then continues from Greenfield Dock along the edge of the estuary past former small ports at Bagillt and Flint, and through the newly created Bettisfield recreational site, to the 13thC Flint Castle. It follows a new section of the Wales Coastal Path being developed by Flintshire County Council's Coastal Unit. As the Dee is a RAMSAR site of international importance for nature conservation, please pass through sensitive areas at high tide quickly and quietly to avoid disturbance to roosting birds.

1 From the middle of the High Street turn into Tower Gardens. At its end descend steps, go through the underpass and along the left-hand side of the car park. After the pelican crossing follow a meandering pathway down into Greenfield Valley. Go under the arched bridge passing the site of Holywell station. *Built in 1869 to serve local quarries, the standard gauge branch line provided a passenger service from Greenfield until 1954. The 'Little Train' as it was known steamed up a gradient of 1 in 27.* Follow the former railway track down the wooded valley past side paths. Eventually the track narrows and crosses a footbridge. Soon afterwards the path descends to join the previous route section by Basingwerk Abbey. Follow it back across the car park and along Dock Road to Greenfield Dock.

2 Here follow the road right, then take a signposted path to Bettisfield/Bagillt along a formal cycle/walkway. Continue on the signposted path, shortly passing an industrial estate. After crossing a narrow creek by a nearby road entrance to the recycling centre, the gated path continues on an embankment along the edge of the saltmarsh (sensitive area). The path then crosses a former industrial site to go through a kissing gate just before the railway line at the head of Dee Bank Gutter. *This small port was once linked to nearby leadworks and a foundry, and briefly in the early 19thC passenger services to Liverpool via Parkgate and Hoylake operated from here. It is known locally as 'The Holy' from the water which gushes from the outlet of the Milwr tunnel, which originally shared the same source as St Winefride's Holy Well – hence its name. The 10 mile tunnel was driven inland from here at Boot End in stages between 1897 – 1957 primarily to drain lead mines in Holywell and Halkyn Mountain, but it also opened up new lead and zinc veins. An average of 23*

37

Greenfield
Dock

A548

Basingwerk
Abbey

B5121

Greenfield

Royal Oak

St Winefride's
Well

A5026

High St

①

Holywell

0 kilometres 1

0 miles ½

N

A5026

Bettisfield

③

②

Bagillt

through the kissing gate and follow a wide path up to an information board at a good viewpoint along the estuary, returning down to another kissing gate further along. The different routes meet then follow a raised surfaced path along the edge of the saltmarsh, or nearby track to reach a footbridge over the railway at the former

A548

million gallons of water flows daily from the tunnel.

Continue along a wide surfaced path to a barrier gate by a high fence compound, containing the former winding house of Bettisfield Colliery (1872-1934) – *the most important of various local coal mines and now a car spares site.* A sign ahead welcomes you to Bettisfield – Gateway to the Dee. From here an option is to turn left along a stony track passing an inlet containing small fishing boats then follow a surfaced path along the estuary edge beneath the main Bettisfield site, soon turning inland. Otherwise follow a raised path ahead above the track round to a kissing gate. Here you can simply continue past wooden sculptures, a nearby car park and track. A better alternative is to go

Bagillt Station
(1849-1965).
Bagillt is an industrial village and small port that developed during the 18th and 19thC, with lead and coal mines, zinc and chemical works, a brewery and rope-making works. The remains of leadworks and large areas of waste testify to this being the most important lead working area along the estuary. The nearby water gutter, now silted, was an important cargo port handling large amounts of coal, lead, zinc and copper.

3 Here bear left to a hidden kissing gate and go along the raised surfaced path, then continue beside the fence beneath the railway line to join the end of the embankment ahead.

Flint Castle

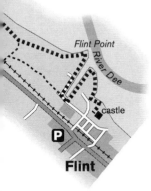

Castle). Just before, follow another path left to a kissing gate giving access to a new wide surfaced path which leads to Flint Point. Continue along the western side of the former Flint Dock – *a long narrow tidal inlet, which for over a hundred years from the early 19thC was a flourishing port trading in local lead, coal and later chemicals* – then an access road to a junction at the entrance to Flint recycling centre. Turn left, then follow the signposted Coastal Path/Castle Walk past an information board at the end of Flint Dock and along its birch-covered eastern side. The raised path then meanders along the tree covered estuary edge to eventually reach a car park by Flint Castle.

Now follow a path along the top of the stone clad embankment gradually becoming closer to the estuary edge. At its end a waymarked path leads towards a kissing gate/gate (offering an alternative path to Flint Dock via birch woodland, signposted to Flint

11 Flint Castle to Dock Road, Connah's Quay

4¾ miles

After a short section of the new Coastal Path the route continues through Flint and Oakenholt, then follows a designated roadside cycle/walkway to Connah's Quay. Flintshire County Council is hoping to extend the Coastal Path across the edge of the saltmarsh as part of a continuous off-road route to Connah's Quay, if sensitive birdlife issues can be resolved. This will greatly improve this section of the Dee Way.

Flint Castle (1277–80) was the first castle built by Edward I during his conquest of Wales. It was strategically placed to secure the ancient low tide ford across the Dee from Shotwick, from where Edward led a great army. It features a Great Tower or Donjon of French influence. Nearby he founded a town encircled by bank and ditch for English settlers, and granted it a Royal Charter in 1284. The capitulation of Richard II to Henry Bolingbroke, later Henry IV, at Flint Castle in 1399, leading to his abdication, is immortalised in a scene from Shakespeare's Richard II. In 1403, the castle was besieged and the town attacked during Owain Glyndwr's uprising against the English. During the Civil War, the castle changed hands several times before finally succumbing to the Parliamentarians in 1646, after which it was dismantled.

By the early 19thC Flint was a flourishing seaport and a fashionable bathing place which became more popular with the the

arrival of the railway. In the 20thC paperworks, flour-milling, and textile manufacturing, came to the town.

As well as oyster-catcher, curlew, redshank and shellduck, the foreshore attracts the entire estuary stock of Pintail duck, overwintering black-tailed godwits, and the twite.

1 After visiting the castle follow the pathway to the road. (To access the town centre via a footbridge over the railway, go along Castle Street ahead.) Turn left, then shortly follow a pathway round the edge of a car park to information boards. Go past the end of the lifeboat station to join a wide cycle/walkway which runs along the estuary edge past the rugby pitch to a junction at the far end of the football ground. The Coast Path currently continues ahead to beyond a nearby viewing area. Look for signs that it extends along the saltmarsh edge. For the time being follow the cycle/walkway right to join a road which crosses the railway line to reach the A548. Follow it out of Flint and through Oakenholt, then continue on the roadside cycle/walkway past the Oakenholt Papermill and along the dual-carriageway, later angling away to a road which leads to the Power Station.

2 Continue along the road ahead to rejoin the cycle/walkway. At a roundabout follow it under the nearby road bridge on the B5129 and past another roundabout. Shortly, the cycle/walkway continues on the right-hand side of the road into Connah's Quay. At the Pelican crossing by Deeside

Liverpool, London, Dublin and parts of North Wales. Shown as 'New Quay' on late 18thC maps, by 1839 it was renamed Connah's Quay, possibly after an Irish merchant or landlord at the Old Quay House. Its later prosperity was then largely due to the export of tiles and bricks directly from Buckley by a single track railway which opened in 1862. It also became an important shipbuilding centre, with Ferguson, McCallum & Baird building steamers and three masted sailing vessels

❶ castle
lifeboat station
Flint
0 kilometres 1
0 miles ½
A548
paper mill
Oakenholt
❷
power station
River Dee
A548
College
Old Quay House
Dock Road→
P
Connah's Quay

College cross back to the opposite side and continue along the pavement past the Halfway House. Just before the Cross Keys, take the signposted path between Capricorn Car Sales and Golftyn church. Follow it to cross a footbridge over the railway line, then alongside the wall to reach a wide pathway. Turn left – *enjoying a good view of the stylish modern road bridge over the Dee* – and follow the pathway close to the railway line, past a play area and buildings, then turn left past the side of the Old Quay House inn (1777) at Connah's Quay. Turn right to reach nearby Dock Road, which you follow left past industrial units to its end at Wepre Riverside car park.

After the new channel was cut in 1737 a stone pier and quay was built at the hamlet of Goftyn. By the early 19thC it had been developed by the Irish Coal Company into a thriving port, from where ships sailed regularly to

between 1859–1917, and James Crichton's yard producing a diverse range of small boats. During the late 19thC a fleet of coastal sailing ships traded to other ports in Britain and Europe. It became the main Dee port and was so busy that ships often berthed alongside each other whilst waiting to load or unload. It was one of the last British ports to own sailing ships. By the 1930s the port had declined due to silting and competition from Liverpool, and about 1960 the docks were closed. The quayside is now much changed, but one original dock remains.

41

12 Connah's Quay to Saltney Bridge

5 miles

This section continues to Hawarden Bridge, where it crosses the river and follows the cycle/walkway along the northern bank of the canalised Dee past the Blue Bridge at Queensferry to Saltney Bridge. The straight, peaceful and little known canalised section of the river has a lot of history to tell. There is an alternative path along the south side of the river.

On the first part of this section to the Queensferry, you will see along the northern side of the river the remains of several wooden wharves associated with the once extensive iron & steel works of John Summers & Sons, now Corus, first established in 1896. During the 20thC it operated a fleet of vessels, many built locally, for shipping steel around Britain and Europe. In 1980 open-hearth steel-making dramatically ended, with the loss of over 6,000 jobs.

Hawarden Railway Bridge, which you soon cross, connected North Wales via the Wirral with Liverpool, and trains still regularly cross the Dee en route between Wrexham and the Wirral. William Gladstone laid the first cylinder of this swing railway bridge in 1887. Two years later his wife Catherine opened the bridge allowing a flotilla of vessels to pass through to the cheers of spectators lining the banks. The bridge consists of two fixed spans, with a central 285 feet span that could be swung open in 30 seconds by two huge hydraulic rams, originally worked by steam driven pumps, later electrically driven.

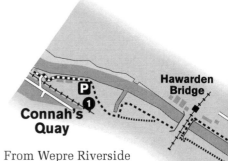

From Wepre Riverside car park go along the cycle/walkway, soon bending away from the river to reach the former Connah's Quay railway line. Here, turn left to pass over the long narrow inlet, then go through a kissing gate on the left on the signposted riverside walk. Follow the path along the embankment on the eastern side of the inlet. Shortly, bend right with the embanked path, past a track and on to rejoin the cycle/walkway. Follow it to Hawarden Railway bridge. Go up steps to cross the adjoining bridge over the river. At the other side, just before Hawarden station, descend steps on your right and walk along the northern bank of the river, passing the former John Summers Steel HQ. Continue along the embanked path passing old wharves and on to reach the road near the Blue Bridge connecting Queensferry and Garden City. Turn right.

The 1732 Act of Parliament that led to the canalisation of the Dee by 1737, required the provision of two ferries across the new channel – Lower and Higher – linked to ancient trackways across the Dee marshes between Flintshire and Cheshire, and both had been established by 1740. Higher Ferry at Saltney was for foot passengers only.

Lower Ferry, established at this point, provided passage for passengers, animals, carts and carriages. In 1820 it was named King's Ferry in honour of George IV's accession, then Queensferry in 1837 upon Victoria's accession. Tidal movements and flooding often made the crossing hazardous, but after the

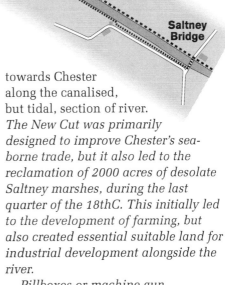

1830s it became much safer after the introduction of a system of chains linked to the flat bottomed boat and each bank. It became an important link between North Wales and Liverpool, and in 1872, an average of over 1000 passengers and 300 carriages a week crossed here.

The demise of the ferry came with the opening of the Jubilee Bridge in 1897. However, it struggled to cope with increasing and heavier road traffic, and in 1926 it was replaced with the Blue Bridge, made of steel and with electric controlled mechanisms able to open or close it in 2½ minutes. The remains of the old bridge are still visible.

2 Cross the road at the Pelican crossing to resume your journey alongside the river. Shortly, you pass

under the 1960 road bridge, and continue above the river.

By the mid-19thC the waterfront opposite was a hive of activity, with warehouses, wharves and tramways linked to local collieries and the potteries at Buckley, enabling the export of coal, bricks, and tiles. Wharves also served a chemical works, wire works and an explosives factory. Shipbuilding flourished during the 19thC and a fishing fleet was based here. Early last century, the sea trade declined, and now only the remains of the wooden wharves remain.

The wide recreational route is unerringly straight as it heads

towards Chester along the canalised, but tidal, section of river.
The New Cut was primarily designed to improve Chester's sea-borne trade, but it also led to the reclamation of 2000 acres of desolate Saltney marshes, during the last quarter of the 18thC. This initially led to the development of farming, but also created essential suitable land for industrial development alongside the river.

Pillboxes or machine gun emplacements are a feature of the

The view from Hawarden Bridge

river from Connah's Quay. They were sited at key locations in 1940 to provide defensive cover. They were made of reinforced concrete with 15 inch thick walls and a 12 inch thick roof. Loophole openings provided a 90 degree field of fire for each of 5 guns, and there was also an anti-aircraft gun mounting. Locally, there was always concern about German aircraft landing on the Dee, so wire hawsers were stretched across the river to prevent this happening. Later you pass on the opposte side of the river a new quay built by British Aerospace to enable Airbus wings, built in its nearby factory, to be transported along the river. Small boats may be seen on this section, including the occasional water-skier. Eventually you reach Saltney footbridge. Go past the front of cottages. *The modern garage of Ferry House is the site of the original ferryman's cottage.*

13 Saltney Bridge to the Old Port, Chester

2¼ miles

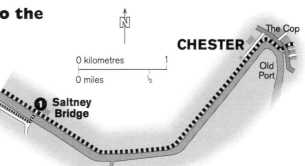

The trail continues alongside the river to The Cop and the site of the Old Port.

Until 1968, when the current footbridge was built, the ferry carried people from Blacon and Sealand road to the many Saltney-based industries, including the aircraft factory at Broughton, and children to school. In the 1950s an outboard motor replaced oar and muscle, and the boat was able to carry 15 people and push bikes. Bob Manifold was the last of several generations of the same family who worked the ferry. In an article, he recalled the times when ships were ice-bound here and at Chester.

The arrival of the railway in 1846 saw extensive industrial development on the southern side of the river leading to the creation of Saltney as a thriving suburb of Chester, and Saltney Ferry as a railway village. The Great Western Railway used tugs to tow up to 300 ton ships up river to its own wharf, where goods such as wheat and iron ore were offloaded and coal and flour exported.

In 1913, James Crichton opened a shipbuilding yard at Saltney, to complement one at Connah's Quay. Both yards produced small vessels of great variety, including tugs, cargo ships, vehicular ferries, lightships, barges, hospital ships, and yachts. The largest was an oil tanker – the Alleghany – of 828 tons built in 1921.

He was an efficient shipbuilder and innovator, and a good employer to his average workforce of 300. Little evidence remains of the yards which closed in 1935 and once built ships that plied their trade throughout the world.

▌ Pass round the end of the bridge to rejoin the river bank, then continue alongside the river towards Chester. Shortly, the river bends – *on the opposite bank is a pillbox and the remains of Saltney wharf* – then continues along a straight section. At the next bend of the river follow the path through the edge of Cop Park – *from where in the 18thC Cheshire cheese was exported to London* – soon bending away from the river to reach Sealand Road. Turn right to reach the Dee Lock, where the canal joins the river by modern apartments at the site of the Old Port.

Here you have a choice of routes through Chester to the Old Dee Bridge: either a riverside route from the Old Port (**A**) or via the city walls from Tower Wharf (**B**). See Section **14**.

CHESTER TO FARNDON
12½ miles

14 The Old Port to the Old Dee Bridge, Chester
1¼ miles

Chester's maritime fortunes

The Romans realised the Dee's strategic importance and built their legionary fortress Deva, now Chester, at the head of its broad tidal estuary. By the Middle Ages the city had become a thriving sea port, maritime centre and strategic gateway for government and trading links with Ireland, and had an important wine trade with France and Spain. Exports included leather goods, Cheshire salt, Welsh cattle and sheep, and even slaves! Local coastal trade was important, especially for supplying the North Wales castles. From the 15thC silting became an increasing problem, which prevented larger boats reaching Chester. Whilst this led to the development of the small estuary ports, Chester retained its role as the administrative port for the area. From the late 18thC shipbuilding became established here.

Unfortunately the benefits of the New Cut were short-lived, and the arrival of the canal connecting the Dee at Chester with Nantwich in 1779 failed to stop its decline as a port, with trade going to the emerging Liverpool. However, Chester's fortunes revived after the canal was extended to Ellesmere Port in 1795, providing a thriving trading route between the Mersey and the Midlands. The canal originally ran into the Dee through a large tidal basin, but in 1801 a separate lock separated it from the river. The Dee Basin, then later Tower Wharf became an important centre for canal boat building and repair. By 1920 Chester had ceased to be an active port.

The Dee used to flow near the western city walls, where there are the remains of a Roman quay, and where the later quays of the Old Port were sited. The river steadily receded and the Water Tower, marked the river's edge when it was built in 1322 to protect the port. Further quays were sited on the south side of the river by the Old Dee Bridge.

There is a choice of interesting routes through Chester.

Route A – via the riverside

The new riverside promenade from the Old Port, past the Roodee and racecourse, to the Old Dee Bridge opens up an historical section of the Dee. Note that the Roodee section of the path will be closed during race days.

From the Dee Lock – built in 1801 to link the river to the Shropshire Union Canal – go along the pavement, then take the pathway between the first two apartment blocks to pass along

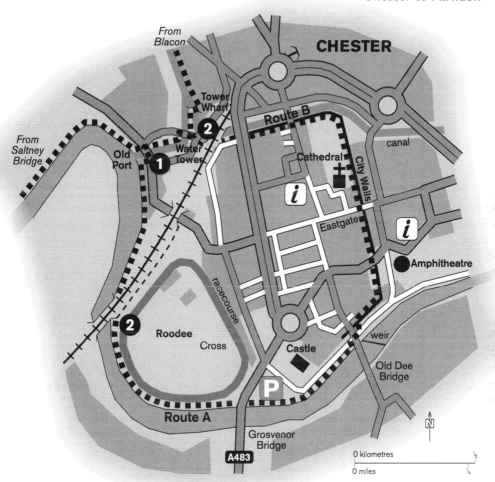

their riverside frontage. Continue to nearby New Crane Wharf, with its old warehouse, where the walkway is built directly above the former quay. *Here sea-going vessels up to 350 tons berthed here after the second half of the 18thC.* The pathway continues above the river, passes under the railway bridge built in the 1840s, then enters the Roodee. *In Roman times this area was a tidal pool and was later named after a small medieval stone cross (Rood), whose base still*

remains. The racecourse, dating from the 16thC, is the oldest in the country. The ancient city walls overlooking the racecourse stand on the original river cliff.

2 Follow the pathway round between the racecourse and the river to pass under the Grosvenor Bridge to reach Little Roodee car park. *Opened in 1832, this stone bridge, with a single span of 200 feet, was the largest in the world. Chester Castle can* *be seen. The original Norman motte and bailey castle was built in 1070 to protect the bridge over the Dee and the port.* Continue alongside the river to reach the Old Dee Bridge. *This section of riverbank by Castle Drive, once had a flourishing leather industry, which during the 17thC employed a fifth of the local population. Alongside the bridge is the former hydro-electric power station, built in 1913 on the site of the 11thC Dee Mills, making Chester the first British city to generate hydro electricity. In 1951 it became a water pumping station.*

Route B – via Tower Wharf and the city walls

This route follows the ancient city walls through the heart of this historic city passing close to the Cathedral and Roman amphitheatre, the largest ever found in Britain. The city walls, a Scheduled Ancient Monument, are the most complete circuit of Roman and medieval defensive town walls in Britain, and regular information boards trace their history. The Romans built them to replace the original wooden defences of the Deva fortress. They continued to play a key role in subsequent periods of Chester's history, then became a fashionable promenade in the 18thC.

1 From the Dee Lock cross the road and take the pathway along the side of the canal basin, past a liftbridge and round the side of canalside apartments to go up steps to a road. Turn right across the canal, then go through a kissing gate opposite and down to the towpath at Tower Wharf, the larger of the two canal basins – with Telford's Warehouse opposite.

2 From Tower Wharf follow the towpath under the road and railway bridges and up past Northgate lock. After passing under a road bridge, go up a cobbled path to pass through an archway in the city walls. Turn right to go up the nearby steps onto the walls at Morgan's Mount. Here, turn right and follow the delightful city walls, soon crossing Northgate Street, with the canal below, before turning past King Charles Tower towards the Cathedral – *built in 1092, on the site of a Saxon church.* Continue past Bell Tower Steps and across Eastgate with its ornate 1897 clock, then Newgate, with the amphitheatre nearby. *The Roman Gardens below were the site of a clay tobacco pipe factory (1781–1917), making Chester centre of a flourishing industry, exporting great quantities.* Shortly the river comes into view. At the Recorder Hotel leave the walls to go down Recorders Steps – *erected in 1700* – then turn right along The Groves – *Chester's popular riverside walkway* – to reach the Old Dee Bridge.

15 The Old Dee Bridge to Aldford

5½ miles

The Dee Way between Chester and Farndon offers the most continuous close riverside walking available on the Dee. This section follows a popular riverside path to the former Eccleston Ferry, with an optional visit to the nearby attractive village of Eccleston. It then skirts the edge of the Eaton Estate, the family home of the Duke of Westminster, before crossing the river by a splendid early 19thC cast iron bridge to visit the attractive 19thC Eaton estate village of Aldford. It is a section of the Marches Way.

The seven arched stone Old Dee bridge was built in 1357, a successor to earlier wooden bridges that have stood here since the late 11thC, near the site of an earlier ford used by the Romans. The bridge was the only crossing over the river until the 19thC and important for trading and military purposes. Tolls regulated traffic across the bridge for centuries until they were abolished in 1885. The river is tidal here.

Across the river, Handbridge was known as 'Treoeth' or burnt town, because it was so often set on fire by the Welsh during frequent clashes with the English. Chester became the base for the conquest of North Wales. Interestingly, an ancient city bye-law, never repealed, prohibits Welshmen from entering taverns or meeting in groups of three or more!

The weir was built in the 11thC to provide the water power for a corn-mill on the Chester side of the

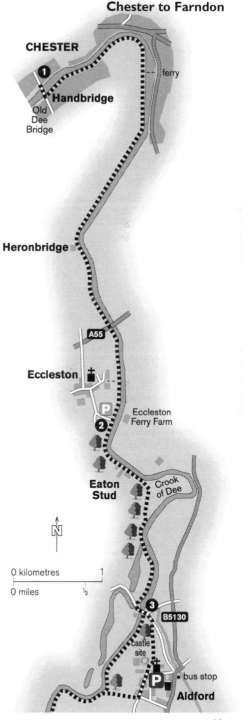

CHESTER

ferry

Handbridge

Old Dee Bridge

Heronbridge

A55

Eccleston

Eccleston Ferry Farm

Eaton Stud

Crook of Dee

N

0 kilometres 1

0 miles ½

B5130

Castle site

bus stop

Aldford

49

bridge, producing flour and oatmeal until the 19thC. Fulling mills for washing cloth were built on the south side of the weir. For centuries the weir was blamed for the silting of the river downstream, flooding and impeding salmon heading upstream to spawn, but survived all attempts at its removal. Steps now help migrating salmon to pass this barrier.

Salmon fishing is one of Chester's traditional industries. The river between the weir and the Dee bridge was known as 'King's Pool' – only the Abbott of Chester and his monks were allowed to fish in it.

Rowing on the river has been popular since the 18thC, but in the 19thC its promotion as an athletic, gentile and innocent sporting pastime led to the establishment of Chester Victoria Rowing Club in 1838 – the oldest 'open' rowing club in Britain. The Queen bestowed respectability on rowing by granting the title of 'Royal' two years later. Other local clubs followed, along with race prizes and betting and the Chester Regatta began in 1863.

I Walk across the bridge then turn left down steps to follow the riverside pathway past a fish-pass and trapping house at the end of the weir. *It was used to tag and monitor the progress of salmon and sea trout to their spawning grounds above Llangollen.* Continue under Queens Park suspension bridge – *built in 1923 to replace one from 1852* – and past rowing clubs on both sides of the river to enter Earl's Eye Meadows. Follow the riverside path round past

elegant houses on the opposite bank and the ferry crossing point, then along the edge of a series of fields. Go past a large pumping station and houses at Heronbridge. *In Roman times there was a crossing here and a quay for discharging tiles and pottery from Holt, for transporting by cart to Deva to avoid the weir.* Continue on the riverside path to pass under the A55. *Ahead lies Eccleston, with its red sandstone church tower.* After going through a kissing gate, a path leading right takes you up to Eccleston, which is well worth a visit. Otherwise continue alongside the river to reach a car park at Eccleston Ferry.

A ferry began here in the mid-18th C to replace a well-established ferry further upstream, and operated until 1940. It was variously known as Eaton Boat Ferry, Eccleston Ferry,and Jemmy's Boat after James Harnett, its ferryman at the end of the 18thC. This section of the river was popular for boating trips in Edwardian times.

2 Continue along the part wooded riverside path. Shortly after passing Eaton Stud the main path bends away from the river through an area of woodland. It then joins a track, which becomes an access lane passing a red sandstone timber-framed cottage. *Note the plaque indicating the water level on February 9th 1946.* As the lane bends right, keep ahead to go through a small gate, and follow the path near the river to eventually reach a road. Turn left across the blue and white cast iron bridge over the river, with views to Aldford Church.

The Old Dee Bridge and Weir, Chester

The Chester-Whitchurch Roman road crossed the Dee here by an ancient ford, from which Aldford gets its name. It was replaced by a free 'Etone Bote' ferry maintained by the lords of the manor, which ran for over 400 years until the mid 18thC, when the ferry moved to Eccleston. The current single 151 foot span bridge was built in 1824 on the Aldford approach to Eaton Hall for Robert Grosvenor, the first Duke of Westminster. At its eastern end is the name of its builder – William Hazedine – who undertook much of the ironwork on the famous Pontcysyllte Aqueduct at Trevor.

3 If you do not wish to visit Aldford continue along the riverside path. Otherwise, go along the road, and at the end of the small wood, turn right to go through a small gate. Head up the field towards the church to go through a kissing gate. *To your right is the remains of Blobb Hill, the 12thC Norman motte and bailey castle, which used to defend the ancient ford and border against Welsh attacks.* Follow the path to the road by the church – *built in 1866 in late 13thC style by John Douglas, the Duke of Westminster's architect, who designed many of the houses of this attractive mid-19thC estate village.* Keep ahead to reach the road junction at the Post Office/shop.

16 Aldford to Farndon

5¾ miles

The route continues along the edge of mainly open fields alongside the tranquil river, later featuring riverside wooden chalets of various designs, and passing through a fish farm. It is less well used than the previous section.

1 Continue along School Lane past the village school. Just after a junction turn right along a lane on a signposted footpath. Go through a small wooden gate and continue along a hedge-lined green track. Just before it begins to bend left, go through a gap on the right. Immediately turn left to follow a path through the trees to the nearby river. Turn left and follow the path near the river to a stile at the end of the wood. Continue round the edge of the next two large fields near the river, often hidden by summer vegetation. On entering a third field, turn right along the field edge. In the corner turn left up the field, then right with the boundary, and in the corner ahead go through a gap.

2 Follow a path back towards the river and along the field edge and through a gap into the next field. Head down towards the river and walk along the field edge, later joining a green track running alongside the boundary on your left. Shortly, you join another track leading into a field just beyond fenced off equipment. Bear right and walk along the field edge. As the path bends with the river, on the opposite bank are the first of a series of wooden chalets. Continue round the edge of the next two fields, then follow the riverside path past a chalet to soon enter woodland. Go past Noonday chalet and along a green track. When it splits keep ahead to reach a finger post. *Nearby is an old ferry crossing linked to Churton, reputed to be a smuggling route across the border.*

3 Continue ahead signposted to Farndon. Follow the path along the wood edge, soon passing behind a chalet before leaving the wood. Go along the edge of two fields, past another chalet (Meg's Place) and along the next field edge to go through a kissing gate. Follow the path to cross a track and go through another kissing gate to pass between chalets. Go ahead along the field edge and through a small gate just above the river. Go through the gate ahead and follow the waymarked path through the fish farm, passing between a green barn and a chalet, then bending right along a track past other buildings before heading back towards the river. Go through a kissing gate to enter a field and continue with the open riverside path. After a few hundred yards head half-left to cut off a corner to rejoin the riverside path. Go through another kissing gate and follow the enclosed path. After a further kissing gate, go along the edge of the next two fields and through another kissing gate by a chalet. Follow a green track passing behind secluded riverside chalets, then the path through several kissing gates to reach the medieval Dee bridge.

Here the ancient communities of Farndon and Holt stand either side of the Dee, separating England and Wales, an important crossing point since Roman times. The present 14thC sandstone bridge, a scheduled ancient monument, was built by monks of St Werburgh's Abbey in Chester, and originally had a gatehouse and chapel. It was once part of the important salt route from Nantwich into North Wales, and tolls were levied for its use for five centuries. Legend says that the ghosts of two young princes haunt the bridge where they were drowned for their inheritance!

Farndon, a small farming community, whose most famous son was John Speed (1552–1629), historian and mapmaker, became embroiled in the Civil War. Between 1643–45 St Chad's Church, dating from the 14thC, was garrisoned by Parliamentary troops. In fierce fighting with the Royalists, based at Holt Castle, for control of this strategic crossing point, both the church and village were badly damaged. After the war, the church was restored, and a new chapel added, containing a small stained-glass Civil War commemorative window dating from 1662. Near the porch is an ancient yew tree, where troops were said to have rested their pikes and swords before entering the church. The outside of the tower contains musket ball holes.

One of the earliest race meetings in the country, drawing large crowds, was held on Farndon Hay to the north-west of the village between 1631–1803, eventually being overshadowed by Chester Roodee.

By the beginning of the 20thC

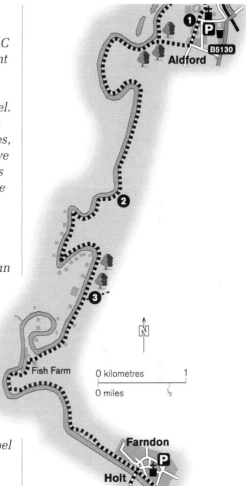

the area became famous for its strawberries, attracting seasonal pickers from the towns.

Holt was originally a Roman settlement, established to provide the garrison at Deva (Chester) with bricks, tiles and pottery, from kilns and a factory built on a 20 acre site near the river. They exploited the available clay/sand deposits and oak forests for fuel. Goods were transported by boat along the Dee, then by cart to

A tranquil river scene

Deva. Nowadays it is better known by visitors for its award winning butchers/ delicatessen and its association with Paul Burrell, the former butler of Diana, Princess of Wales!

FARNDON TO BANGOR-ON-DEE

9½ or 12½ miles

There are two alternative routes following the Dee through the floodplain.

Route A (9½ miles) crosses the river into nearby Holt, then follows public footpaths on the western side of the river, almost entirely within Wales. This is one of the least known and remote sections of the Dee, with no facilities or few dwellings en route. Embankments protect the more vulnerable sections of the river, as it meanders south through farmland for about 6 miles, after which it follows the river Clywedog, before heading south-west to rejoin the Dee for the final riverside path into Bangor-on-Dee.

Route B (12½ miles) follows the eastern side of the river and is different in character, with less sense of remoteness. Whilst providing sections of quality riverside walking at the beginning and the end, it takes a line above the flood plain to visit a 12thC church and the small rural communities of Shocklach and Worthenbury, where there are country inns. The initial route to Shocklach lies in Cheshire and follows the waymarked Marches Way. Soon after Shocklach Hall it enters Wrexham County Borough and continues via Worthenbury to Bangor-on-Dee.

Whilst both routes offer easy walking on good field paths, in summer you are likely to encounter occasional rotational maize fields (sections 18 and 20) within the Wrexham Borough Council area. The Highways Department agreed, in early 2011, to send a letter to relevant landowners to remind them of their responsibility to ensure paths are not blocked by crops. If you encounter any problems the Council will like to hear from you (01978 292057) so that further action can be taken.

Medieval bridge connecting Farndon with Holt

Route A
17 Farndon to
Old Lower Hall

3¾ miles

I Cross the old bridge over the Dee from Farndon to enter Holt and Wales. Walk through the village, passing St Chad's Church. *The attractive sandstone church, dating from 1267 was used by Parliamentary troops for stabling their horses during the siege of nearby Holt castle.* As the road bends right into the village centre, go straight ahead along Castle Gardens, signposted to the castle, passing the former Holt Endowed School 1874–1977. Follow the enclosed footpath down to reach an information board at the site of Holt Castle.

Holt Castle was built around a block of Triassic sandstone 245 million years old between 1281–1311 following the conquest of Wales by Edward I. During the Civil War the castle, occupied by Royalists withstood a year long siege, before falling in 1647 to Parliamentary forces who then marched into Wrexham. It was then partly demolished and in the late 17thC, stones were taken down Dee by barge for building of Eaton Hall.

Go past the castle remains and through a kissing gate. Continue ahead, soon alongside the river, to reach another kissing gate. Follow the track ahead under the road bridge and on to a kissing gate on the left above the river. Follow the riverside path round the edge of a large field to a kissing gate in the corner to rejoin the track.

2 Turn left to cross a stile, then bear left to rejoin the river, shortly crossing a stile. Continue near the river, over another stile, then round the riverside edge of the next large field to go through a gateway. Follow the river round the edge of the next field to cross a pair of stiles. Now angle away from the river across the middle of the large field to go through a gate near the far corner. Continue ahead across the field, past a Cheshire waymarked gateway, and on alongside the boundary, with the river now nearby, to go through a facing gate in the corner.

3 Turn right alongside the fence to cross a stile, then angle left to follow the river embankment to a stile/ gate. Continue beside the river, then after about 50 yards keep ahead, moving away from the river embankment. About a further 70 yards, just past a hedge/tree boundary corner to your right, turn left to cross a stile in the tree boundary. Pass to the left of a small pool and continue to a gate ahead near the river. Follow the river embankment round to cross a wooden section of fence in the boundary. Now go across the large field to rejoin the river embankment just before the far field corner. After going through a gate go half-right across the large field to cross a Cheshire waymarked wooden fence in the boundary about 30 yards to the right of a gate near the early 18thC Old Lower Hall. Continue to the garden fence corner ahead by the access track. Keep ahead alongside the fence, across another track, and on to a small gate beyond.

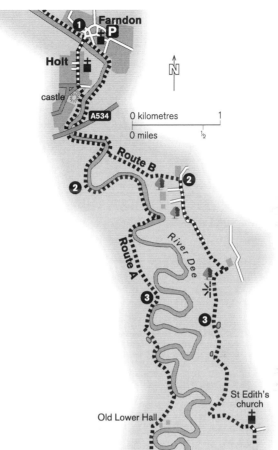

Farndon

Holt

castle

A534

Route B

Route A

River Dee

St Edith's church

Old Lower Hall

The Dee by Old Lower Hall

18 Old Lower Hall to Bangor-on-Dee

5¾ miles

1 Continue ahead, soon leaving the river embankment to cross a stile in the boundary ahead. Go straight across the maize field to a cross-track by the embanked bend of the river. Keep ahead across the next maize field, passing under electricity cables, to cross a stile in the boundary on your right just before the corner. Head across to join the river embankment, then where the river and embankment bend, angle left across the maize field to a gate in the far corner. Follow a green track to a waymarked stile near the bend of the river. Go half-left to follow the flood embankment to cross a gated stone bridge over a stream.

2 Now go slightly right across the large field to cross a pair of stiles in the corner. Head to the left to join a fence by the river embankment. Continue beside the fence, soon bending left. After a few yards angle away from the fence to cross a pair of stiles in the tree boundary ahead. Go ahead across the large field to rejoin the river, then follow it right to a stile near a gate – *a delightful place for a break*. Continue above the river, over another stile, and on along the long field edge to a stile in the corner. Keep ahead, past a field flood embankment, and follow the riverside field edge round to a stile beyond the other end of the flood embankment. Go round the next embanked riverside field edge to cross a stile.

3 Continue with the flood embankment, leaving the Dee to accompany the nearby river Clywedog, soon visible. When the embankment bends away from the river towards a wood, head half-right to a stile in the field corner to enter the wood. Follow the waymarked path through the wood passing near the river to cross a stile at the wood edge after about 150 yards. Turn right and continue near the river. Shortly, cross a gated bridge over the river, then go along the edge of a field and a wood to reach a road at Orchard Croft. Turn right, then left along another hedge-lined road. After about 300 yards take a signposted path on the left through a gateway. Go slightly right across the field, then after passing a farm to your right, continue down the long field's right-hand edge.

4 At the bottom corner, turn right through a gateway into the adjoining field. Keep ahead across the field to go through a waymarked gateway. Angle left across wettish scrubland to follow the hedge boundary on your left to a stile in the corner. Go along the right-hand field edge to a stile in the corner. Continue ahead along the field edge, then cross a stile on the left. Turn right, then head towards the old tree-covered railway embankment to pass under the twin arched bridge. Turn right, then angle gradually away from the railway embankment to cross a stile in the boundary ahead to rejoin the Dee. Continue past a small pumping station, then briefly follow a track, to cross a stile by a gate ahead. Go along the riverbank, then pass round the left-

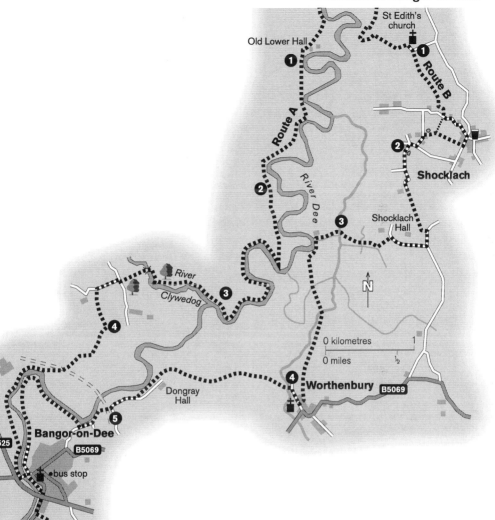

hand side of a larger pumping station and continue to a kissing gate. Follow the tree-lined riverbank to cross a gated bridge over a stream. Now head down the long field, then go through a large gap in a tree boundary on your left just before a pylon, then follow the riverside path to the old bridge at Bangor soon visible ahead. Cross the bridge into the picturesque ancient community of Bangor-on-Dee.

Route B
19 Farndon to
St Edith's Church
4 miles

1 From the old bridge go down into Farndon Picnic area and through the car park. *Note the nearby red sandstone Dee Cliffs, an SSSI, created from sandy sediment deposited during the Triassic period, some 250–252 million years ago.* Continue along the riverside track, then path. Shortly, when the boardwalked path bends inland, continue along the riverside path through several fields – *later with the ruin of Holt Castle visible opposite* – to eventually pass under the A534. Continue with the riverside path. After crossing a stile at a waymarked path junction, bear right near the river alongside a line of tall poplars. Shortly, at a finger post, turn left away from the river along the field edge. After about 150 yards you join a rough hedge/tree lined farm track, later improving, which you follow to a road by farm buildings.

2 Turn right along the quiet country lane, later passing Oakwood Traditional Furniture. When the lane ends at Crewe Farm, keep ahead along a short hedge-lined track to enter a field. Keep ahead to enter a larger field and follow the hedge round to cross a stile. Keep ahead along the next field edge to another stile. Continue to the hedge opposite and follow it right to a stile/gate in it near the field end. Keep ahead alongside the fence. *The river Dee is hidden below as it meanders across the flood plain.* Near its end angle right to the hedge corner ahead and follow the hedge to a stile/sleeper bridge. Follow the waymarked stiled path across two fields.

3 In the next field angle right to a hidden stile in the hedge by a small pool. Turn left along the field edge to a stile in the corner. Go half-right to follow a faint green track past another lilly-covered pool. Just beyond angle left to a stile/sleeper bridge in the boundary. Go across the field and through a large gap in the hedge ahead. Go slightly right across the next field to a sleeper bridge/stile in the tree boundary corner ahead. Bear left to join a farm track which descends to a stile/gateway. Continue ahead across the next field to cross a stile in the far right hand corner. Although the next stile is a little further south along the boundary, the right of way now heads half-left, crosses a stream and pastureland, then does a sharp U-turn back across the stream to the stile. Go up the field to a stile in the top corner onto a green track. Cross the stile opposite, then follow the boundary on the right round to a stile in the corner and go up the side of the churchyard to pass St Edith's church.

This delightful sandstone church, with its Norman south doorway, was built about 1150. It is now isolated from the original border settlement of 'Socheliche' that existed around a motte and bailey castle ½ mile to the north.

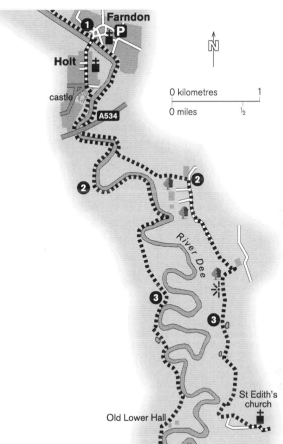

St Edith's Church

20 St Edith's Church to Bangor-on-Dee
8½ miles

I Go through the kissing gate and turn right along a lane. On the bend, keep ahead past a small building to a stile. Go ahead across the field to a stile/sleeper bridge/stile at a fence corner. Continue ahead across the next field to a stile/sleeper bridge by a pool. Keep ahead along the field edge, and in the corner angle left to a waymarked gate. Turn right, then left to follow the field edge round to a stile. Go ahead across the large field to cross a stile and another ahead. Follow the field boundary round to cross a sleeper bridge/stile and go across the next field to join a lane. Follow it left past Newhouse – *note the stone gargoyles on the barn and nearby stocks* – then the school to reach a T-junction opposite the 19thC Bull Inn in Shocklach. Turn right past an 1898 milestone and the village hall. Take the signposted path between Thursday's Cottage and a barn to cross a stile beyond a garage. Follow the stiled path along the edge of two fields, then past the left side of a pool – *in summer covered in yellow flowers and lillies* – to join a lane by White Cottage. Follow it left, past other dwellings and an old water pump, then at the junction turn right.

2 At a lane/track crossroad, turn left along a track past a house. When it splits, go through the gate ahead. Later, after the track bends right, go through a waymarked gate on the left and follow a green track past the house to go through a gate by outbuildings and a small pond. Go through the right of two gates ahead, then through a nearby waymarked gate on the left. Turn right along the edge of the large field to a stile/sleeper bridge in the corner at a waymarked path junction. Keep ahead to follow the field edge round to a stile to join the road. Follow it right, then turn right along the no through road. Follow it past Shocklach Hall, with its extensive red-bricked outbuildings – *soon with views over the flood plain to Worthenbury*. Take a signposted path over a stile on the left. Go down the field edge to cross a stile in the corner. Go across the field and through a gate ahead. Cross the farm track beyond and go through another gate just ahead. After passing the bend of a water channel continue across the large field to cross a waymarked stile in the boundary ahead by the bend of another water channel.

3 Enter the field beyond, then continue ahead along the embanked field edge to a ruin. Go through a gate and cross the footbridge over the water channel into a field. Follow the field edge above the bend of the Dee – *a welcome sight after miles of farmland*. Sadly the encounter is only brief, for you continue along the field edge to go through gates in the corner into another large field. Bear left, angling away from the fence to a stile in the far boundary. Cross the water channel and keep ahead across the next field to a small waymarked gate. Cross the footbridge over Worthenbury Brook and keep ahead along the next field edge to a gate.

Head down the large field towards Worthenbury church to a stile by a telegraph pole. Now follow the stiled path through three further fields, then past the rear of houses to emerge on the road opposite St Deiniol's church. *Dedicated to the Welsh Saint Deiniol, the church was built in 1739 to replace an earlier church, part funded by the Puleston family, an ancient local family. Follow the road out of the village.*

the left of a telegraph pole, to cross a stile in the boundary ahead. Now head half-left across the reedy field towards distant buildings to a stile between corners of the far boundary. Go slightly right across the large field to a concrete water trough at its far side. Angle left to the end of a fence, then head towards two facing gates to the right of the farmyard of Dongray Hall. Go through the waymarked left gate, then across the field to go up steps onto the flood embankment above the Dee. Follow the embankment to a stile in the hedge at Dongray Hall's driveway entrance. Continue along the lane.

4 Shortly, cross a bridge over the river and a stile just beyond. Turn right to cross a stile in the boundary ahead. Go slightly left across the next field to a stile/footbridge/stile in the boundary ahead. Again go slightly left across the maize field to a single old gatepost in the far boundary giving access over a stream into the next maize field. Keep ahead, passing to

63

The medieval bridge, Bangor-on-Dee

5 After 250 yards, on the bend, cross a stile by a gate and go under the former railway bridge. Keep ahead towards a house to cross a stile above the river. Walk along the flood embankment past the house, over a stile, and on to its end. Descend onto the adjoining lane, then go through a kissing gate on the right. Cross the embankment ahead by concrete steps, then head half-left across the field to a kissing gate beyond a pylon near the river. Continue near the river, later angling away to another kissing-gate. A popular local path now continues along the riverbank, but the right of way follows the river round further inland to another kissing-gate. It then angles right to go through a large gap in the tree boundary ahead, and continues to a kissing gate by the river. The delightful riverside path continues to another kissing gate, then follows a gated track to reach the Royal Oak near the old Dee Bridge in Bangor.

BANGOR-ON-DEE TO CHIRK

13¾ or 14½ miles

21 Bangor-on-Dee to Overton

6¼ miles

This section passes through attractive undulating countryside linking the two ancient border communities. It includes some riverside walking, and an opportunity to divert across Overton Bridge, an important crossing point over the Dee, to The Cross Foxes, a 17thC coaching inn, whose riverside garden offers a splendid setting for a break.

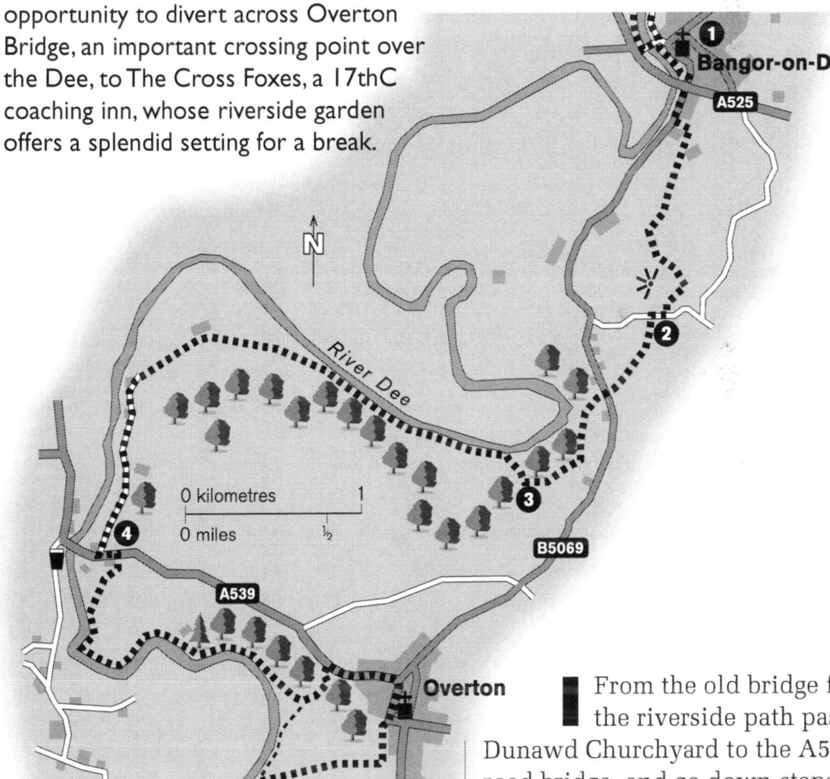

monument. It replaced an earlier wooden bridge and a ferry. The red sandstone early 14thC church was dedicated to St Dunawd, a notable Abbot at the large ancient monastery that existed nearby, before its monks were massacred by the Saxon king Aethelfrith in 615 AD.

Bangor is an attractive village famous for its racecourse, established after an initial race to settle a wager between two local gentry in the 1850s. The present bridge, of medieval origin, but largely 17thC, is a scheduled ancient

From the old bridge follow the riverside path past St Dunawd Churchyard to the A525 road bridge, and go down steps to the B5069. Follow it right past the entrance to Maes y Groes, then take an access lane on the left to pass Althrey Lodge Cottage. Just before Davro, turn right along a short stiled path to a field. Follow the waymarked stile path across two fields, then follow the boundary on your left to cross a stile in the corner. Go half-left across the field, soon rising to a stile and continue up the next field past a tree. After about 150 yards angle right, then bear right past the further of two small pools. Continue across the field to a stile in the boundary ahead onto a lane. Turn right.

2 After 75 yards take a signposted path through a gate on the left. Head almost half-right across the large field for about 250 yards to a stile in the hedge on your right. Go half-left across the next large field to a gate onto a road. Go through the double gates almost opposite and continue to a stile/small gate in the far left-hand field corner. Go along the edge of two fields past a wood. After a stile follow the boundary to a small gate/stile ahead to enter the wood.

3 Follow the path down through the trees to a stile/gate by the river. Continue near the river through the edge of two fields, then a wood. After leaving the wood by a gate, angle gradually away from the river across the field to a stile/gate in the recessed boundary ahead. Go along the next field edge to a stile/gate in the corner near extensive farm buildings, then angle left along the field edge to join an access lane. Follow it past houses to the A539. (A short diversion right will bring you to Overton Bridge and The Cross Foxes.)

This bridge dates from 1816 and followed two earlier bridges, which

had a ford further downstream, but had proved to be expensive to maintain. In 1790 a coach approached the bridge too fast and the horses, coach and passengers plunged into the river. Cross Foxes, built in 1681, was an important staging post on the Chester – Shrewsbury coaching road, where horses were changed and travellers took refreshments. Coracle fishing was popular until the 1920s and annual coracle races were held near the bridge, attracting large crowds.

4 Cross the A539. Turn left, then just past the entrance to Isa-bella, turn right along a farm track into a field. Turn right passing behind the houses, then continue round the edge of the large field. Later you join the river and pass a weir, with a former water mill on the opposite bank. The path then bends with the river to a stile/gate and continues through the edge of a wood, leaving it by a gate. Go along the field edge to waymarked double gates in the corner. Go through the next field to more double gates near the river, then follow the track along the wood edge. After a stream and just before gates, take a path on the right to a stile. Walk along the field, soon moving away from the river onto higher ground to follow a path angling inland towards houses on the wooded skyline to cross a stile/sleeper bridge at the tip of the wood. Follow the main path up through the wood to eventually emerge onto the A539 (caution). Cross the road with care and walk along the pavement into Overton. After passing the attractive terraced Dispensary Row

Dispensary Row, Overton

– reputedly named after one of the cottages was occupied by a succession of district nurses – follow the road into High Street.

Overton, named as 'Ovretone' in the Doomsday Book, was given to Robert Fitzhugh by William I. Edward I, who had twice visited Overton, granted it a Royal Charter in 1292. It had a motte and bailey castle built by Prince Madoc of Powys Fadoc, but its precise location is uncertain. It stands on an old drovers route from Wrexham to the Midlands and the South, and in the 18th/19thC was an important mail coach staging point on the Chester-Shrewsbury road. For centuries until the 19thC, when it boasted 8 inns, it was an important market centre, with weekly markets on its wide High Street. St Mary's church dates from the late 14thC but was remodelled in 1870. Its famous yew trees dating back to medieval times are included in the Seven Wonders of Wales. One fenced tree is between 1500-2000 years old.

22 Overton to Flannog Farm

4 or 4¾ miles

The sections Overton to Chirk (7½ or 8¼ miles) follow part of the long established Maelor Way and the new Wat's Way to rejoin the Dee, passing the ancient ferry crossing point at Erbistock, before continuing across attractive part wooded countryside. Later the trail heads towards the historic border town of Chirk.

I Continue down the right hand side of the High Street past the White Horse coaching inn and St. Mary's church. As the main road bends left, turn right on the signposted Maelor Way. Follow the lane down to a gate at its end by sewerage works. Continue along a track, then after crossing a stream follow the embanked green path between two large fields to reach the tree-lined banks of the Dee. Turn left along the field edge to cross a footbridge in the corner. Follow the path through the riverside edge of Llan-y-cefn wood to cross a stile into a field. Continue through the field to another stile in the corner, then follow the riverside path through woodland. *Soon visible on the opposite bank is the 19thC St Hilary's church at Erbistock.* You then pass the former ferry crossing point to the Boat Inn opposite, on the site of an old ford. *The winch on the opposite bank was used to pull a small boat across the river until 1939.* Continue with the riverside path through the trees, crossing a large footbridge.

2 Towards the end of the wood the path bears left. After a few yards turn right off the main path and follow another path down to cross a large footbridge over Shell Brook. This bridge has been dislodged by high floods, and Wrexham Borough Council are striving to stabilise and secure it to allow for the Maelor Way to be re-opened. The Council also hope to improve the next section of the route by establishing a higher level permissive field path to the lane than the original shown. It will be clearly waymarked with kissing gates. Afterwards follow the lane south to reach a delightful timber-framed house, the former Sodylt Old Hall, dating from the 14thC, with the larger Sodylt Hall nearby. (If this section is still closed, an alternative route is to continue with the main path above the wooded side valley to eventually join an access track which takes you to the B5069. Follow it right, then take a no through road on the right. At a junction bear right. After passing Sodylt Hall, the road bends left past outbuildings to Sodylt Old Hall at point **3**.)

3 Go along the track opposite. The high hedge-lined green track soon narrows, then descends and becomes more a tree-lined path, which eventually ends at a field gate. Keep ahead across the field to another gate, then continue along an enclosed green track. *Soon visible ahead is 17thC Pen-y-lan.* Later you pass barns at Plas-yn-y-coed to reach its driveway. Go through the gate ahead by a Maelor Way finger post, then turn right along

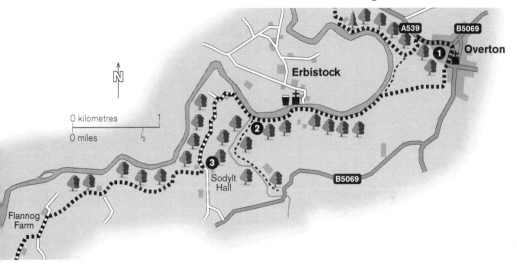

the field edge, soon passing wooden fencing to go through a waymarked gate. Turn left and follow the path down into a small wooded valley and on to cross a footbridge. The path rises and continues near the wood edge to go through a gate into a field. Go past a few nearby trees, then go slightly right up the large field to a stile by a large water trough. Go up the next field past a large tank to go through a gate in the right-hand corner by Flannog Farm.

The Boat Inn, Erbistock

23 Flannog Farm to Chirk

3½ miles

1 Turn left up the access lane. After about 250 yards at a bend, turn right to follow a path into trees and along the woodland edge – *soon reaching a fine high viewpoint across the Dee valley towards Castell Dinas Bran, Ruabon and Llantisilio Mountains.* Shortly, at a cottage you join a lane, which you follow past two houses to a T-junction. Here cross a stile on the right. Follow the boundary on your left down to cross a stile in the field corner. Go down the next field to cross a stile in the bottom left-hand corner. Work your way along the rough bottom field edge to pass a pylon, and on to cross a stile amongst holly in the boundary ahead. Descend to the lane and go up the stepped path opposite to a stile into a field. Follow the waymarked stiled path along the edge of three fields to enter a wood. Follow the path through the edge of the wood, later descending to pass an outbuilding to join the nearby lane by Woodside.

2 At the far end of the house you leave the Maelor Way by turning right to follow an enclosed path down through the trees past two houses to cross a footbridge to reach a road. Follow it right for ⅓ mile to cross a bridge over the river Ceiriog, then cross a stile on the left. Angle up the field to a stile by a gate. Continue ahead up the next field to a stile in the top corner at the right-hand side of a small wood. Go past the fence corner ahead and continue across the large field to a stile in the hedge onto a road. Follow it left for ⅓ mile to go over the A483. At the T-junction, turn left (Chirk) then go through a kissing gate on the right. Now follow a stony path across Chirk Green – *once the site of a colliery and now reclaimed for community use* – ignoring side paths to leave it by a gateway to reach a road just ahead. Turn left past the fire station. At the junction, turn right and follow the road to a T-junction in the centre of Chirk. Turn left along the main road to the Hand Hotel opposite the war memorial.

Chirk, known in Welsh as Y Waun, meaning 'The Moor', stands in Wales overlooking the border with England. Its strategic importance is evidenced by a 12thC Norman castle and the more famous Chirk castle to the west completed in 1310 by Roger Mortimer for Edward I after the conquest of Wales. The castle, now a National Trust property, was occupied by the Myddleton family since 1595. Running through the castle grounds is Offa's Dyke built about 790 AD.

Chirk is also situated on Thomas Telford's historic London to Holyhead turnpike road, along which stagecoaches carried the Irish Mail. Coalmining has played an important part in the development of the town and surrounding area since the 16thC to 1968 when the last local colliery closed.

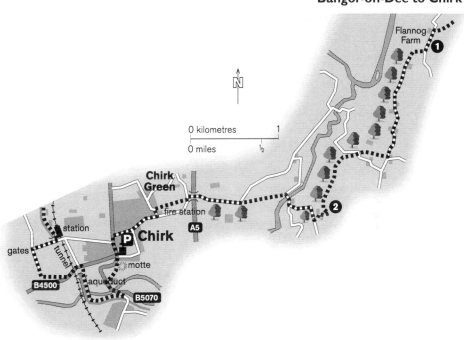

Chirk Aqueduct

CHIRK TO LLANGOLLEN
9½ or 11 miles

24 Chirk to Trevor Basin
5 or 6½ miles

This section features some of the finest examples of canal and railway engineering infrastructure in Britain, including Thomas Telford's famous Pontcysyllte aqueduct, which it is hoped will shortly be awarded World Heritage Site status. The trail heads towards the more rugged Dee Valley via the late 18thC Shropshire Union Canal, one of the most popular cruising canals in the country. It crosses Telford's splendid Chirk aqueduct, offers an optional extension to Chirk Castle, and passes through a short canal tunnel (handrail – but torch useful). There is then a choice of routes to Pontcysyllte aqueduct and Trevor Basin: **Route A** features Ty Mawr Country Park with its Visitor Centre, a 19thC railway viaduct and a delightful section of riverside walking. Shorter **Route B** continues with Offa's Dyke Path along the canal to make an exhilarating crossing of the aqueduct high above the Dee.

❙ From the Hand Hotel, an early 19thC coaching inn follow the main road through Chirk past St Mary's parish church, parts of which date from the 12thC. *Behind The Mount, the prominent 18thC three storey house on the corner, is the remains of an early 12thC Norman motte and bailey castle which protected the ford over the river Ceiriog. In 1164 it resisted Henry II, whose army was subsequently defeated by the Welsh at Crogen 2 miles to the west of Chirk.* Continue down the pavement on the B5070 to cross a stile on the left. Follow the path down the hillside to cross a stile by an old leat and on to rejoin the B5070 at the entrance to Seventh Heaven, a former mill. Turn left along the pavement, soon crossing the river Ceiriog. Cross the road with care to the Bridge Inn and continue up the road to reach the Llangollen canal at bridge 21. Here turn right and walk alongside the canal, past cottages and across the aqueduct over the Ceiriog valley.

This splendid 10 arched structure carrying the canal 70 feet above the Ceiriog valley was designed by Thomas Telford, the great engineer, and completed in 1801. Nearby is the railway viaduct built by Henry Robertson in 1846-48 for the Chester-Shrewsbury railway line. It was built deliberately higher than the aqueduct to emphasise the superiority of rail over water! Due to the objection of Col. Robert Myddleton Biddulph of Chirk Castle it was built at night! Both are built of local yellow sandstone. At the other side you enter Wales. Ahead is the entrance to the ¼ mile long Chirk tunnel which, being narrow, means boats travelling in opposite directions cannot pass.

2 Take the path angling up to the road. Turn left and go along the B4500 towards Glyn Ceiriog. Shortly take a path angling off the road on the right through trees, then follow the perimeter of a caravan park round to its entrance. Continue along the road to a junction by impressive early 18thC ornamental wrought-iron gates and screen. *Known locally as 'The Pretty Gates', they were made by the Davies brothers of Bersham and originally stood at the north front of the castle. Further along the road ahead is the start of a waymarked 1 mile permissive footpath (1st April – 30th September) to Chirk Castle – well worth a visit if time allows.* Go down the road signposted to Chirk.

3 After passing a signposted path go through a gap on the left to follow a path angling down to the canal towpath near the northern entrance to Chirk tunnel. Continue along the towpath initially through the wooded cutting and later passing a marina. After 1½ miles go through the 174 metre Whitehouse tunnel, guided by a handrail, to the exit clearly visible ahead – *perhaps accompanied by a narrow boat illuminating the tunnel with its headlight!*

4 After emerging from the tunnel you have a choice. For **Route B** simply continue along the towpath to Trevor Basin. For **Route A**, turn sharp right to follow a path up to the A5. Turn left along the protected pavement. At the road junction turn left. Follow the lane down past houses and when it bends left go through a kissing gate on the right. Go through the nearby gate and head up the field

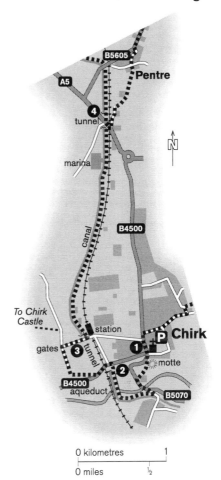

towards Scots pines to go through another kissing gate. Follow the hedge on your left through three gated fields and another kissing gate to reach a road junction in Pentre village. Continue straight ahead to follow the road down past Sun Cottage (1723) to the B5605. Cross the road and turn right.

5 Follow the pavement to cross the Dee into Newbridge – *so named after an earlier 15thC bridge here, which had replaced two previous bridges and a chain operated ferry further downstream.* Continue along the pavement through the scattered community, then at an 1826 Baptist chapel, turn left along Cae Gwilym Lane. Go through the railway viaduct archway and follow the road to Ty Mawr Country Park. *The nearby Cefn area was once a hive of industry with an ironworks and a colliery.*

6 Go through the entrance, then turn left down a tarmaced/stony track. Shortly, turn right to follow a stony path past a dovecote, soon passing close alongside Cefn Viaduct. *Standing 147 feet high, with 19 arches, the viaduct, which carries the Chester–Shrewsbury railway line, was built in 1848 by Henry Robertson. One of the first trains across, full of VIPs, apparently broke down and was stranded in the middle overnight!* The path bends away from the viaduct to run alongside the river. *Side paths allow access to the river for a good view towards the viaduct.* Just before the stony path bends up right, at a footpath sign, go through a gate and descend steps, then follow the riverside path along the edge of a meadow – *in the distance can be seen the aqueduct* – later bending away from the river to reach a gravel track.

Here turn left over a bridge, go past a large brick building, then follow the wooded riverside path to the base of the aqueduct. Follow the stepped path up alongside the aqueduct piers to the canal. A short diversion onto the aqueduct is recommended. *From it you can see the 17thC Bont bridge over the Dee.* Follow the towpath into Trevor Basin, where refreshments are available at The Telford inn.

Trevor Basin was an important area of industrial activity and transport during the early 19thC. The canal was used to transport processed limestone from nearby Froncysyllte as far as the Midlands, where it was used as flux in iron-smelting. It remains a busy service point supporting recreational canal traffic.

The Pontcysyllte Aqueduct, referred to as 'the stream in the sky' is one of the engineering wonders of the world. Built by Thomas Telford between 1795–1805, it carries the canal 126 feet above the River Dee in an iron trough 1007 feet long, 11 feet 10 inches wide, and 5 feet 3 inches deep, supported by 18 stone piers, built of Cefn sandstone. The cast iron was cemented together with Welsh wool boiled in sugar and lime mixed with ox blood. The aqueduct was originally built to extend the canal to the Dee at Chester, but this never happened due mainly to difficult terrain and rising costs. 8,000 people witnessed its opening ceremony.

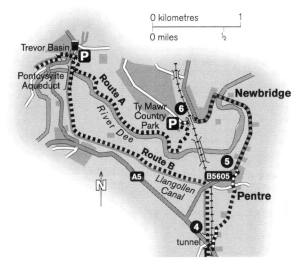

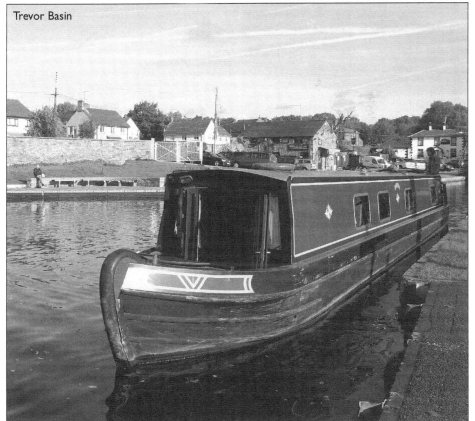

Trevor Basin

25 Trevor Basin to Llangollen

4½ miles

This section offers either a high level route (**A**) on the northern side of the Vale of Llangollen with extensive views, or a slightly shorter easy low level route (**B**) following the canal – a poor weather option. **Route A** follows the waymarked Offa's Dyke Path from the canal to go up through Trevor Hall Wood and along a scenic upland minor road known as the Panorama Walk, passing beneath the impressive limestone escarpments of Trevor Rocks. It then leaves the National Trail to follow a path up to the romantic ruin of 13thC Castell Dinas Bran standing at just over 1000 feet above the valley, with impressive 360 degree views, before descending to Llangollen.

1 Cross the large footbridge over the canal at Trevor Basin and angle left to pass through a gateway (locked at 5 pm) to reach the road. Turn left, then take the path along the canal, soon crossing the footbridge to the opposite bank. (For **Route B** simply follow the canal towpath to Llangollen Wharf, before descending to the town.) For **Route A**, shortly cross another footbridge back over the canal, then go up the field to cross a stile at the top. Follow the path under the old railway line and on to reach the A539. Turn left along the pavement opposite and, shortly, turn right along Trevor Hall Road. On a bend by Gardener's Lodge, follow Offa's Dyke Path along an access track, then half-right up through Trevor Hall Wood, along the edge of a field, and on through a plantation.

2 At a waymarked path junction, take the Offa's Dyke Path down through the conifers. After the next waymarked junction the Offa's Dyke Path contours through the forest, then rises through mixed woodland to cross two stiles, before leaving the trees below a cottage. Continue up the path, soon bearing right up to the cottage's access track, which you follow up to a minor road. *A nearby seat makes a good stopping place offering excellent views along the Dee valley to Llangollen. Dominating the skyline to the west is Castell Dinas Bran and impressive limestone escarpments.* Follow this scenic high-level road, appropriately named the Panorama Walk, enjoying the extensive views and delightful limestone scenery. At a road junction keep ahead beneath Trevor Rocks.

3 At the next junction, you leave the Offa's Dyke Path, by turning left down the narrow lane. At an information board, go through a kissing gate and follow the waymarked path up the steep eastern slopes of Castel Dinas Bran to reach the castle ruins.

The castle, now a spectacular and romantic ruin, with many legends associated with it, occupies a prime strategic position on top of a steep isolated hill overlooking Llangollen and the Dee Valley. Built on the site of an Iron Age fort, the castle is believed to have been built about 1260 by the Welsh Prince, Gruffydd ap Madoc. The castle had a very short life for by 1277 it had been deliberately abandoned

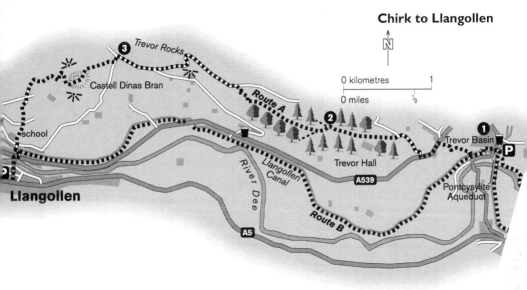

0 kilometres 1

0 miles ½

and burnt to prevent its use by Edward I's invading army. An English garrison was placed there, and despite its subsequent return to Welsh ownership, the castle was never rebuilt.

From the south-west corner follow a clearly marked zig-zag path down the western slopes. As the path begins to level out go up the short slope ahead and on across a small grass plateau. Pass another information board and go down a stony path and through a kissing gate. Follow a track down, across a track/lane crossroad, to a kissing gate at a house. Continue down the field edge to a kissing gate below a lane, and follow the fenced tarmaced path down past a school to a road junction. Continue ahead over the canal at Llangollen Wharf and down the road to the A539 by a taxidermist shop. Cross the road and take the bridge over the Dee into the centre of Llangollen.

Llangollen has developed around

a natural crossing point of the river. A wooden bridge was erected here in 1284, but the present bridge is attributed to Dr. John Trevor, Bishop of St Asaph and dates back to 1346. An additional arch was added in 1861 to accommodate the railway. The town gets its name from St Collen, who established a church here in the 6thC, on the site of the existing 13thC church. During the 19thC textile mills developed nearby on the banks of the Dee, the last one closing in 1967. It was an important staging post on the London–Holyhead coach route and has been a mecca for tourists and eminent travellers since the late 18thC attracted by the area's stunning scenery. George Borrow, the famous travel writer, spent several enjoyable months here in 1854, recounting his walking excursions in the book 'Wild Wales'. Nowadays visitors are also attracted to the town by specific events such as its famous annual International Eisteddfod and canoeing competitions on the river.

LLANGOLLEN TO CORWEN
15½ miles

The route continues more or less on the waymarked Dee Valley Way, a linear Denbighshire County Council promoted walk between Llangollen and Corwen.

Running along the valley is the former Ruabon–Corwen railway line, which opened in 1865, and extended to Barmouth in 1869. This branch line was a lifeline for the scattered rural communities, and important for transporting local slate, timber, livestock and general goods, as well as bringing visitors into the area. It finally closed in 1968, and the track was removed. After considerable voluntary effort, steam trains once more run along this beautiful line between Llangollen and Carrog, and will eventually extend to Corwen.

26 Llangollen to Rhewl
4 miles

The route follows a delightful section of canal, used in summer by horse-drawn narrow boats, to its source at Horseshoe Falls. From the medieval church at Llantisilio it continues through the small hamlets of Llandynan and Rhewl to the Sun Inn, a delightful 14thC drovers inn.

■ Go over the Dee Bridge, and at the junction cross the road. Turn left, then take the signposted tarmaced path, soon angling up its left fork to reach the canal towpath near Llangollen Wharf. Now simply follow the towpath for 2 miles to Horseshoe

Falls – the crescent shaped weir built by Thomas Telford for diverting water into the Llangollen Canal.

On the way you pass the Pavilion where the famous International Eisteddfod is held each July, a Motor Museum, a white water section of the river popular with canoeists, and the Chain Bridge Hotel, with dramatic views of steam trains arriving at Berwyn Station high up above the Dee. The Hotel dates from the 1870s replacing an earlier inn built around the time the first chainbridge was constructed in 1814 by a local coal owner to carry coal across the river from the canal to the Holyhead road. The original bridge and a later replacement were victims of heavy floods. The current suspension bridge was built in 1929. Nearby is King's Bridge built across the river and canal in 1902-6.

From Horseshoe Falls continue alongside the river through kissing gates, then follow the path up to Llantisilio Church. *Built in the 15thC, the church's features include a fine medieval roof, a rare medieval oak eagle lectern, and a sculpted font. The poet William Wordsworth once read a Sunday sermon here.* Go up its access lane, then turn left along the road. After about 150 yards, cross a stile on the right. Keep ahead to another stile then follow a faint green track to a stile on the left. On entering the field, go

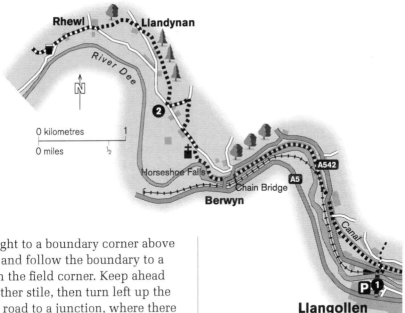

half-right to a boundary corner above a gate and follow the boundary to a stile in the field corner. Keep ahead to another stile, then turn left up the minor road to a junction, where there is an information board.

2 Turn right to go up nearby steps and over a stile. Follow the green track up towards a wood and round its perimeter, then continue across the field. At a waymarker post, go half-left to cross a stile. Turn left and continue alongside the boundary, over another stile and on through the trees, then alongside a fence above a house. At the fence end keep ahead for a few yards, then continue through the trees alongside an old fence to a stile. Follow the wood boundary down to reach a road in Llandynan. Go along the road past a telephone box, then take a track angling down on the left, signposted to Rhewl. Go past a converted chapel and down a path to a kissing gate. Go down the field, through another kissing gate, and on over a footbridge. Follow the hedge, then go through the waymarked gap into the adjoining field. Turn right and follow the field edge round to a kissing gate to descend steps onto the road. Turn right along the road, past the Conquering Hero – *a former inn, built in 1871, and now a community centre.* At Rhewl, take the right fork, signposted Cymmo, to reach the Sun Inn just ahead.

27 Rhewl to the bridge over the Dee, Glyndyfrdwy

4¾ miles

The route now involves several ascents and descents, as it meanders through the foothills and attractive south-facing side valleys of the Llantisilio Mountain range, reaching a height of over 1000 feet, before descending via scenic road and Dee Valley Way link path into the valley to the bridge over the Dee at Glyndyfrdwy. You are never far from the sights or sounds of the Llangollen Steam Railway.

1 Continue along the road past cottages, soon climbing steadily up the edge of an attractive side valley. When the road splits, go down the left fork, soon crossing a stream and passing beneath Acer Ddu. *In nearby fields it was said that hundreds of Prince Llewellyn's army were killed here by Henry III's forces in the 13thC.* Go past the turning for Bwlch-y-Garnedd and on up the lane. When it bends towards a farm, go up the green track ahead. After a stile, continue up the track to cross a stream. Just before an old gateway, go up the sunken tree-lined track ahead. Later, climb up onto the left bank and walk alongside the old track.

2 At the top of the track go through an old gateway and follow a path up through the bracken alongside a fence on your left to go through a gate at a multiple finger post. *There are good views looking back. Between the two highest heather-covered peaks*

in the nearby Llantisilio Mountains is Moel y Gaer Iron Age hillfort. Bear half-left to join the boundary ahead. Now follow a bridleway alongside the fence, steadily descending the edge of the scenic valley to eventually reach a lane just beyond a gate. Turn right, then right again at the junction. Follow the lane to Wern-ddu, then continue along a track which shortly bends down left and crosses a stream. Soon after a gate the green track swings right, goes through another gate then rises up the wooded slope to a further gate onto a crossroad of tracks. Here, turn sharp left and follow the track up to a lane. Follow it right up to a junction. Turn left towards Glyndyfrdwy and follow this scenic high-level road with good views, shortly descending to cross a cattle grid. Here the Dee Valley Way is joined by its link path from Glyndyfrdwy. My route follows neither at this point.

3 Take the left fork of the road junction just ahead. Follow the minor road down to a farm to join the Dee Valley Way link path. On the bend go through a gate below and descend the field edge to a stile in the corner. *Ahead is a good view of the railway line and Glyndyfrdwy, and you may be lucky enough to see a steam train going along the valley.* Keep ahead to descend the gorse and bracken covered slope to reach a solitary wooden post after 100 yards. Continue down the path, soon angling half-right down through birch trees to go through a small wooden gate. Descend the edge of the field to a gate near a house onto a road. Follow it right, shortly reaching

the high bridge over the river leading
to nearby Glyndyfrdwy.

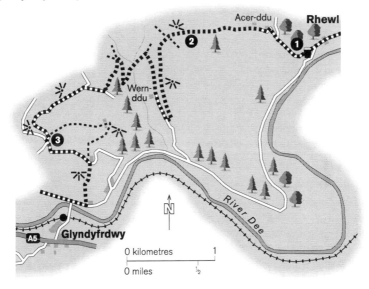

Horseshoe Falls

28 Bridge over the Dee, Glyndyfrdwy to Carrog

3¾ miles

The route now follows the Dee Valley Way up side valleys and across upland pasture, reaching a height of over 1100 feet, with extensive views. It then descends for an additional short section of riverside walking before reaching the picturesque riverside village of Carrog.

1 Continue west along the minor road to rejoin the Dee Valley Way at the next junction. Keep ahead (signposted to Carrog), then just after the entrance to Craig-y-Rhos cross a stile on the right. Go up the field edge to a stile in the top corner and another just ahead. Descend the field edge to cross a footbridge over a stream, then a stile. Now go half-left up the next field and through a gap in the top corner. Continue along the top field edge, over a stile, then follow the narrow bridleway ahead to reach a lane by a derelict farm. Turn right and follow this delightful quiet country lane up past a house. Where the lane begins to descend, cross a stile on the left, and follow the Dee Valley Way up the delightful gated green track to eventually cross a stile at its end.

2 Keep ahead across the field to cross a stile near a pool, often dry in summer. Go half-left to reach an old quarry. Go round its left edge and on down to a stile. Follow the stony track down the hillside, shortly bending left through a gate, and angling down between conifers. When it swings sharp left, keep ahead up another track to a telephone mast. Continue ahead down a path for about 50 yards to go down a long flight of steps and over a stile. Go half-right down the steep slope to follow a broad green track down to a road. Follow the road left to gain access to a riverside path – *too enjoyable to miss* – that will bring you back to the stile opposite. Continue along the road to reach Pont Carrog, the five span stone bridge across the Dee dating from 1661.

The original small settlement here was named Llantsantfraid Glyndyfrdwy – 'the Church of St Bridget in the valley of the Dee'. With the arrival of the Ruabon – Dolgellau railway in 1864, the hamlet was renamed 'Carrog', and rapidly grew in size. A distinctive feature of the village are the tall Victorian and Edwardian houses, built primarily as holiday homes for wealthy families from Liverpool. The area is associated with Owain Glyndŵr, one of the hero's of Welsh history, who led a sustained campaign against English rule at the beginning of the 15thC. His moated manor house was situated across the river just east of Llidiart-y-Parc.

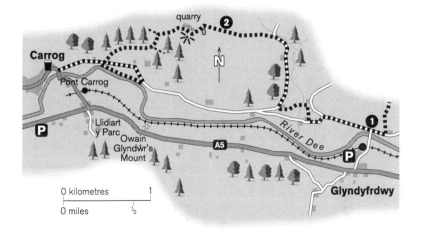

Carrog
quarry
2
Pont Carrog
N
Llidiart y Parc
Owain Glyndŵr's Mount
River Dee
A5
1
Glyndyfrdwy

0 kilometres 1
0 miles ½

Pont Carrog

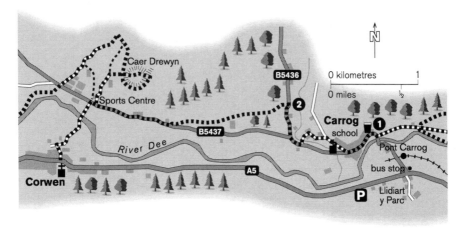

29 Carrog to Corwen

3 miles

The route continues on the Dee Valley Way along quiet roads and paths to Corwen, an historical market and coaching town.

1 Continue ahead through the village past the Grouse Inn, the only remaining one of an original four village inns, and the village stores. At a road junction, turn right (signposted Caer Drewyn) and follow the road past the church, school and old farm buildings, then take the left fork. Follow the road past Felin Carrog Mill to a T-junction and turn right. At the next junction turn right and continue up the road.

2 After about ⅓ mile go up a stony track on the left below a house. Just beyond the track end, bend sharp left on the waymarked path to cross a stile. Walk along the bottom edge of the wood to cross a stile into a field. Follow the boundary on your left up past a wood and down to go through two gates in the field corner. Follow the track past a stone barn to cross a stile ahead. Continue across the field to cross a stile in the far corner, then go half-left down to join a green track. Follow it right to a road. Turn right along the road – *soon with Corwen visible ahead* – to reach a junction near Corwen Sports Centre, just beyond a track signposted to Caer Drewyn hillfort, the next stage of the trail. Turn left and follow the road ½ mile into Corwen.

The ancient community of Corwen was once an important crossing point for traders and drovers, then a key stopping place on the stagecoach route, now the A5, to and from Ireland via Holyhead. After the arrival of the railway in the mid 19thC it developed as a flourishing market town.

CORWEN TO LLANDRILLO

9½ or 12½ miles

30 Corwen to Cynwyd

5½ miles

An early highlight is a short climb on a final section of the Dee Valley Way to visit Caer Drewyn, an impressive Iron Age hillfort with panoramic views, before following a path alongside the Dee to Pont Corwen. It then continues on the former Corwen-Cynwyd railway line alongside the river to visit the medieval Llangar Church, then after further delightful riverside walking reaches Cynwyd village.

Caer Drewyn, a Scheduled Ancient Monument, is a late 1st millennium BC. Iron-Age fort occupying a commanding and strategic position overlooking several valley routes. An early small enclosure was later superseded by a larger fort with extensive stone ramparts which extended down the slope of the hill. It was said to have later been used by Owain Gwynedd and Owain Glyndŵr in their struggles against the English monarchy.

Return along the road to the junction near the Sports Centre. Turn right, then left up a track signposted to Caer Drewyn hillfort. When the track ends at a house, keep ahead to cross a stile. Now follow the signposted path, initially zig-zagging, up the hillside to join a track at a finger post. Follow it up to the top of the hillfort. At a waymark post turn left through the fort entrance to reach a small cairn at its highest point. Now either return down the track or descend the fort's large interior to the finger post. Follow the track down to a signposted track junction by gates and turn right. Cross a stile and walk along the hedge-lined track. Shortly, turn left and follow a green lane, later tarmaced, past Corwen Cutting to the

Llangar Church

B5437. Go through the gate opposite at a finger post signposted River Dee. Go half-right down the field past a pylon to go through a gateway in the bottom corner. Follow the fence along the edge of two fields above the river.

2 Go through a facing gate, turn sharp left and follow a waymarked path angling down the slope, then across a stone slab bridge over a stream and on to cross a stile into a field. Turn left and walk at first alongside a fence, then a boundary of large stones, through two fields close to the river to reach the A5 at Pont Corwen – *the longest bridge over the Upper Dee, built in 1704.* Cross the road and proceed with care over the bridge to cross a stile on the right at the junction with the B4401 to Cynwyd/Llandrillo. Follow the short path (Cynwyd/North Berwyn Way), then turn right along a stony track. Shortly cross a stile to the right of the gated entrance to Troed-y-Bryn. Continue along the bottom edge of landscaped gardens near the river to a stile/gate and walk through the trees on a section of the former Corwen to Bala railway line – *closed in 1964,*

and now managed by Denbighshire Countryside Service as a nature reserve.

3 At a signposted path junction by a house, go through the kissing gate, along a track, then through a gate on the left to visit the late 13thC Llangar Church in its idyllic setting. Return to the kissing gate and cross the stile opposite. Follow a faint green track down to cross a stream, then keep ahead across the large field to cross a stile near the confluence of the Dee and the Alwen rivers. Walk along the field edge close by the river, passing the remains of a footbridge, to go through a gate near a ford in the river. Continue along the field edge, through an old gateway, and on alongside the embanked field edge by the river. About 100 yards before the field corner angle away from the river to go through a gate and over the railway embankment to cross a stile opposite. Follow the old boundary on your right along the edge of three fields, then an enclosed path up to the road. Turn right to reach the centre of Cynwyd.

31 Cynwyd to Llandrillo

4 or 7 miles

This section takes you further along the Upper Dee Valley on a choice of routes to Llandrillo, lying on the former Corwen-Bala turnpike road beside the river Ceidiog which flows into the Dee. **Route A** is a 4 mile walk following quiet lanes, paths, and tracks across the wooded edge of the valley, reaching a height of just under 800 feet. **Route B** is an exhilarating higher level 7 mile walk following delightful ancient tracks around the foothills of the Berwyn Range, reaching a height of 1600 feet and offering panoramic views. These once served as important highways across the Berwyn Mountains that separate the Dee and Ceiriog valleys.

Route A

From the Post Office/store continue along the B4401 road past the Prince of Wales, then take the lane on the left. Follow it across the river, then immediately turn left to follow a narrow lane rising steadily above the wooded side valley. About 50 yards after passing a farm, take a signposted path over a stile on the right. The short tree-lined path leads to another stile then continues across a field passing close to a wood on your left. Just before its corner the path moves away from the fence to cross a stream and goes through a small gate above. Continue across the next field to cross a stile in the right-hand corner. Turn right along the lane past Pant y Gai cottage to take the left fork to reach another narrow lane.

2 Cross the barred stile opposite, then go down to cross the stream. Angle left up the field to another barred stile. Keep ahead past gorse

B4401

Route A

Route B

River Dee

① Cynwyd

②

③

Hendwr

P

Llandrillo

0 kilometres   1

0 miles   ½

N

Route B

Pont Rhyd-yr-hydd

③

and bracken to reach a waymarker post by a large tree. Continue across the grassland plateau before gently descending to another waymarker post on the left. Follow the path through bracken to go through a kissing gate. Ignore the adjoining stile and continue ahead alongside the forest. Soon after a stile follow a green track to a road. Go down the green track opposite on a steady descent to a farm. Continue along its access lane then follow the minor road for ½ mile to the B4401. Follow the road left. After ¼ mile turn right along a lane and just beyond an old barn turn left along an enclosed track, passing a smaller barn.

3 On a bend, cross a stile on the left to enter Hendwr caravan site. Continue along its edge then cross a footbridge over the river. Just past the toilet/utility block, turn right, then left to follow a track past caravans. Cross an access lane and go through a gate ahead. Go past a large barn then angle left to go through a gate by another barn. *The nearby imposing 18thC house reflects the importance of the Hendwr estate, standing at the junction of ancient valley and mountain routes. For many centuries it has been associated with prominent Welsh families.* Continue ahead past a modern house to go through a waymarked gate beyond trees. Now follow a waymarked stiled path through several fields, then go along a short hedge-lined green track to cross a stile near a house. Angle LEFT across the large field to cross a stile by sewerage works, and another just beyond. Follow the lane past the school to the 18thC stone bridge over the River Ceidiog in Llandrillo.

Route B

1 Follow instructions in section **1** of **Route A**.

2 Turn left and follow the narrow lane up to its end by Henfaes Issa. Continue ahead up the gated green track, soon rising steadily up the hillside. After another gate it becomes enclosed and contours across the slope to join a road. Keep ahead, passing a large barn, where the tarmac ends and becomes a track which offers easy walking and extensive views. After a gate by Scots pines the track climbs steadily, before contouring towards the flanks of the Berwyn Range and crossing a cattle grid. Shortly the track descends to a gate before meeting another stony track by a metal post.

3 Here bend sharp right to follow this track down past a a strip of forest to cross the old stone bridge of Pont Rhyd-yr-hydd. *A path on the left leads to a nearby waterfall and commemorative slate seat – a delightful place to stop.* Continue up the track and on past a plantation. This delightful open gated track heads back towards the Dee Valley then contours across open pastureland. At a crossroad of tracks keep ahead and follow the gated track on a steady descent. After passing above Ty'n-y-cae-mawr the track becomes more a path which descends through trees to join a lane which you follow down into Llandrillo.

LLANDRILLO TO Y BALA

9 miles

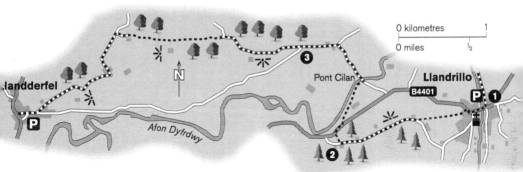

32 Llandrillo to Llandderfel

4¾ miles

The route now follows the southern edge of the narrowing valley before taking a riverside path to Pont Cilan, where the Dee is crossed. It then rises up the attractive wooded hillside on the northern side of the valley, reaching a height of about 800 feet, before descending to Llandderfel.

1 Continue through the village past attractive 18thC cottages, the Dudley Arms Hotel, and the entrance to the 19thC Parish Church. Just beyond the village stores on the main road to Y Bala, go through a metal kissing gate on the left. Follow the track to a lychgate giving access to the cemetery. Continue along the path to go through another kissing gate. At the wall corner turn left parallel with the cemetery boundary and go across the field to a stile. Go across the next two fields to reach a green track. Cross the stile almost opposite. Go up the field to

a stile in the top boundary and follow a narrow path up to a lane by Tyn-y-Ffridd. Continue up the lane and follow it past several houses.

2 Just past Llechwed Celan, take the signposted path through a gate on your right down the field and through a narrow strip of woodland to the B4401. Turn right along the road and after 150 yards cross a stile at the wood corner opposite. Now go half-right to reach the tree lined boundary above the Dee. Follow it along to a stile near Llawr-cilan. Continue above the river to reach a minor road by Pont Cilan. Cross the bridge and follow the road past the old railway line. At a junction turn left and follow the road up past old farm buildings.

3 When the road splits take the right fork. The lane rises steadily then briefly more steeply. After ½ mile, after passing through a gate the lane bends right. Here keep straight ahead on the higher of two green tracks, soon

Llandrillo

descending gently to cross a stream to go through a gate. The green track soon rises past a small wood, goes through a gate and passes a side track on your left. *Soon you have a view ahead of Arenig.* Follow the track past Cai Pant farm and then its access lane to a road. Turn left and follow this quiet road as it descends in stages to the outskirts of Llanderfel where you join another road. Follow it past toilets and across the stream. Now bear right on a side lane past cottages to reach the main village road by the telephone box. Turn right past the village stores and the 15thC church.

Llandderfel takes its name from St Derfel Gadarn, a famous 6thC warrior-saint. In order to promote Christianity, he adopted the same powers as Cernunnos, the pagan god of Nature and the Underworld, who had stag antlers on his head. In the Middle Ages many pilgrims came to pray to his large wooden image, often bringing animals to be cured and blessed. The tradition that the image would set forests on fire was strangely fulfilled, when in 1538, on the orders of Thomas Cromwell, who wanted to root out superstitious practices, it was removed and publicly burned at Smithfield, London, along with Friar Forest of Greenwich, who was accused of high treason. His wooden stag, without its antlers, is all that remains of the famous shrine and now stands in the church porch. However, it continued to play an important role in village life. Each Easter Tuesday, it would be carried in procession to a hill near St Derfel's Well and then converted into a ride for local children.

33 Llanderfel to Pont Bala

4¼ miles

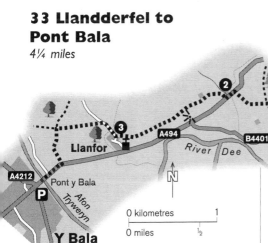

The route now follows a quiet lane rising north west, before turning along a bridleway past an attractive upland lake, at a height of about 900 feet, with extensive views. It then descends the attractive wooded hillside towards the distant Llyn Tegid before heading to the ancient community of Llanfor and on to cross Pont Bala at the edge of the historic market town of Y Bala.

From the church continue up the road out of the village, then turn left on a road signposted to Cefn-ddwysarn. It rises steadily, passing Ty-newydd. After ½ mile, when the road bends sharp right, continue ahead along the access track leading to Ty'n-y-bwlch – *enjoying extensive views of the Berwyn mountains to the south and the Arans to the west*. Follow the track past Llyn Maes y Clawdd – *a small upland lake, which provides fishing and bird-watching facilities specifically for people with disabilities* – to go through a gate and on past the house to gently descend to go through the right hand of two gates. Keep ahead along the edge of the long field – *with views of distant Llyn Tegid* – to a stile in its corner. Now follow a stiled path down and alongside the wood boundary to reach an old farm. After passing between buildings turn right on a waymarked path along a track and follow it up to a cottage. Go through a gate ahead by a shed, then another on the left about 25 yards further. Go ahead across the field's mid-slope to a gate in the second corner. Continue ahead with the stiled path through two further fields to reach the A494. Cross the road with care, then walk left along the verge. *The mound on your right is Tomen-y-Castel.*

2 Just past the entrance to the bunkhouse barn turn right up a track on a signposted path. Keep to its left fork and follow the track to a house. Go past the front of the house and through a small white gate. Cross a stile beyond and continue ahead up the field and along its edge past a small wood to go through a gate in the corner. Follow the boundary fence on your left down the field – *enjoying a stunning view of the Dee, Y Bala and Llyn Tegid, with the Arans and*

Cader Idris beyond – to cross a stile in it. Angle gently away from the fence down to go through a reedy area and on past an old gate post ahead. Go through a wide gap in a nearby boulder wall corner and continue along the field edge just beneath the boulder boundary. In the field corner go through the waymarked wooden gate and follow the permissive path near the fence on the left to cross a stile at its end. Go slightly left across a track to a small wooden gate, then follow a track to reach the road in Llanfor.

A nearby gate gives access to the village church. Built in 1875, it stands on the site of the oldest church in Merionydd. Among the intricately carved headstones is the grave of a man who survived 27 battles, including Waterloo. The large stone building at the top of the churchyard is the mausoleum of Richard John Lloyd Price of nearby Rhiwlas Hall, a famous sportsman, author and founder of a short-lived Welsh whiskey distillery. It was paid for by a wager on the horse Bendigo that won the Kempton Park Jubilee in the year he died-1887 – hence the inscription above the doorway: 'As to my latter end I go to seek my Jubilee, I bless the good horse Bendigo, who built this tomb for me'.

3 Turn right through the village, over a stream, then continue up the road to take a signposted path through a gate on the left. Now walk through a delightful narrow area of attractive mature trees, known locally as the 'Lovers Walk'. At a facing wall cross a concrete stile on the left. Keep ahead to follow the stiled path down and along the edge of two fields to reach an enclosed pathway adjoining the A494. Follow it right. After crossing a lane and passing the old arched gateway leading to Rhiwlas Hall you cross Pont y Bala over the Afon Tryweryn to enter Snowdonia National Park and Y Bala town. Its centre lies along the road ahead.

Y Bala – meaning 'the outflow of the lake' – has a beautiful setting on the shores of Llyn Tegid, the largest natural lake in Wales, surrounded by hills and mountains. It lies on a natural fault that has provided an important route into the heartland of Wales since prehistoric times, and later became part of the Roman road system. The town was created in 1310 by Roger de Mortimer to reinforce English control of the district, but despite its English origins, Y Bala is a strong Welsh-speaking community that has produced renowned poets, politicians and preachers, who have helped to shape cultural and religious life in Wales, and further afield in Patagonia. In the 18th and early 19thC the town was renowned for its knitted woollen gloves, stockings and caps. Today, it retains its status as a small market town for the local farming community, and as a centre of the Welsh language and culture.

Y BALA TO LLANUWCHLLYN

7 or 8¼ miles

The trail continues through part of the southern area of Snowdonia National Park, across the hills and open upland pastures above Llyn Tegid, offering good views of the lake and surrounding mountains, to Llanuwchllyn. After an initial walk from Pont y Bala alongside the Afon Tryweryn to join the Dee and reach the edge of Llyn Tegid, the route splits into two equally attractive alternatives. **Route A** passes along the end of the lake, then heads across the hills on its north west side – a section adopted, upgraded and waymarked by the Snowdonia National Park Authority. **Route B** meanders across the foothills on its south east side, enjoying more extensive views of the lake throughout, with opportunities to see steam trains on the Bala Lake Railway. It may also be partly waymarked at some time in the future.

Llyn Tegid, 4 miles long, nearly ¾ miles wide, and up to over 140 feet deep, is the largest natural freshwater lake in Wales. The river enters the lake at Llanuwchllyn as the Afon Dyfrdwy and is said to pass through 'without mingling the standing waters'. The lake contains the unique gwyniad – a whitefish member of the herring family imprisoned here after the Ice Age, when the lake was formed. Llyn Tegid is rich in legends. One says that the lake is named after the mythical prince, Tegid Foel, whose town was one night engulfed by the huge lake in vengeance for his cruelty to his subjects. Another is that the valley was flooded after the keeper of St Gywair's holy well, forgot to replace the lid.

34 Route A

8¼ miles

1 After going over Pont y Bala, immediately cross the road to a small gate opposite, then follow the signposted path along a wide grassy embankment parallel with the Afon Tryweryn. Pass a weir, cross a road, and continue on the green embanked path close by a section of the river. After passing another weir, the path angles away from the Tryweryn to briefly join the Dee before reaching the B4391. Cross the road.

2 Turn right and follow the pavement along the nearby side road passing along the end of Llyn Tegid. At a car park, take a tarmac path which runs near the shoreline of the lake, enjoying the view along the lake to the Arans. Eventually, you pass behind the Leisure Centre and Tourist Information Centre, then above a lakeside car park to reach the A494 by Loch Café. Follow the pavement above the tree-lined edge of the lake to Fronfeuno car park. Continue along the pavement. Just beyond the Llanycil road sign cross the road and go through the Fron Feuno farm entrance gateway on a signposted bridleway. [From here you will be following the Snowdonia National Park Authority waymarked route to Llanuwchllyn.

Follow the track up to a finger post on the bend. Here, go half-left to follow the waymarked path beneath trees along the top field edge to cross a stile in a fence corner. Follow the path through the wood then up the right-hand edge of a long reedy field to a finger post at the top.

3 Bear left, then angle away from the boundary down to cross a stile/footbridge. After a small gate go up the field to another small gate, and across the next field. Go through a gate and on between cottages. Cross the caravan site's driveway and go up the lane ahead past a house to a stile. Go across the undulating field to cross a stile below the final rise. Go towards the farm to cross a ladder-stile and continue ahead along a green track to cross a sleeper bridge and ladder-stile. Go down the field edge to cross a ladder-stile near farm buildings. Go briefly ahead, then bear right up a green track to cross a ladder-stile. Head towards a distant house and a ladder-stile just beyond. Go across the moorland towards a small plantation, past a finger post – *with a good view of Arenig* – to cross a footbridge/stile at the plantation corner. Walk round the edge of the plantation and along the field edge to a road. Follow it left.

4 After ⅓ mile take the signposted path over a stile on the right. Go along the field gradually angling away from the fence to a stile. Now follow the stiled waymarked path through several fields to a farm. Pass to the left of conifers and buildings, following a green track up to a ladder-stile. Keep

ahead, soon following the boundary on your right to cross a ladder-stile near the fence corner. Go half-right to follow telegraph poles down to a ladder-stile. Descend steeply to a ladder-stile below onto a track. Follow it left round past Llwyn-mawr-isaf, then follow its driveway, later alongside the river, to the road. Turn left, then right through a gate by cottages. Now follow the SNPA's waymarked permissive route up Tyn Llechwedd's access track to a finger post, where the track splits.

5 Follow the right fork past sheepfolds up through a waymarked gate. Follow the track through another gate. On the bend, keep ahead on the signposted path along the reed and gorse covered edge of a cleared forest, near the fence – *with good views of the Arans and Cader Idris* – to cross a sleeper bridge then a stile at its end. Continue ahead across the large field to go through a gate in the far left-hand corner. Follow the signposted path by the fence to a stile. Keep ahead along the bottom of the slope soon descending to a stile by the stream/plantation. Continue down the edge of reedy terrain to cross a stile and footbridge on the right. Follow a track to a lane by Erw Fron.

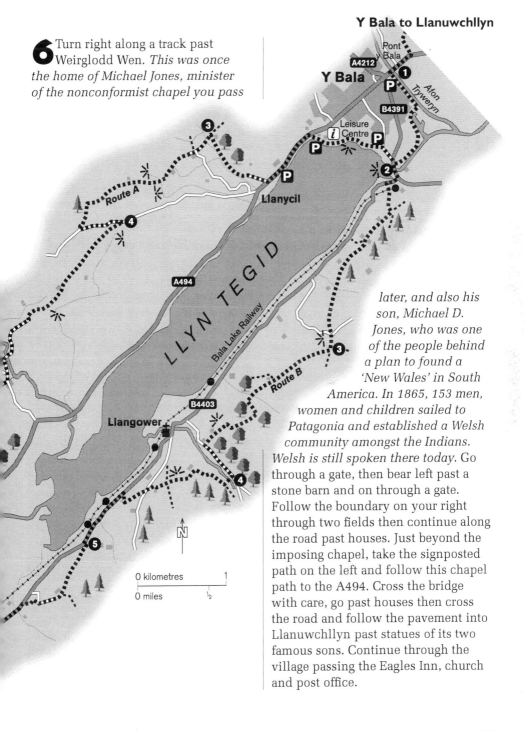

6 Turn right along a track past Weirglodd Wen. *This was once the home of Michael Jones, minister of the nonconformist chapel you pass*

later, and also his son, Michael D. Jones, who was one of the people behind a plan to found a 'New Wales' in South America. In 1865, 153 men, women and children sailed to Patagonia and established a Welsh community amongst the Indians. Welsh is still spoken there today. Go through a gate, then bear left past a stone barn and on through a gate. Follow the boundary on your right through two fields then continue along the road past houses. Just beyond the imposing chapel, take the signposted path on the left and follow this chapel path to the A494. Cross the bridge with care, go past houses then cross the road and follow the pavement into Llanuwchllyn past statues of its two famous sons. Continue through the village passing the Eagles Inn, church and post office.

95

35 Route B

7 miles

1 Follow instructions in section **1** of **Route A**.

2 Turn left, soon crossing the point where the Dee emerges from the lake. Go over an old stone bridge to the B4403. Go through the kissing gate opposite at the entrance to Bala Lake Railway. Follow the path to the platform and cross the footbridge over the railway, then follow a stiled path up two fields to reach a track. Follow it right, past farm buildings and on past the rear of Bala Lake Hotel. Go through its front car park and just beyond a cattle grid, take the waymarked path on the left angling up the slope. After a stile the path crosses the bottom slope of a field past a house, before rising past a wood corner and continuing alongside a fence. At its corner the path bends right down towards a cottage, then rises and continues alongside the boundary to a stile. It then heads up the bracken-covered slope, soon bending left and continuing across the open hillside, enjoying extensive views. The path crosses a stream and continues up to cross a road and a ladder-stile in the fence above. Continue up the track to cross another ladder-stile at a superb viewpoint.

3 Follow the delightful green path angling down the bracken-covered hillside. At the bottom, follow the fence on your right past a ladder-stile to eventually cross a ladder-stile near a sheepfold, a stream and a ladder-stile opposite. Continue ahead across the field for about 100 yards to cross another stream (it may be dry). Now turn left and follow the stream up the hillside to reach a waymarked tree by a section of old wall. Turn right and follow the waymarked path alongside the fence, which it briefly leaves then rejoins. After a small gate, follow the fence down through two larger gates to a house. Follow the waymarked path behind the house, then go down its access track to a road. Follow it left along the attractive wooded valley.

4 Shortly, take a signposted path angling down on the right to cross a footbridge just upstream of a concrete bridge. Follow the path back to the concrete bridge and go up the stony track. On the bend, keep ahead to follow a path up to a ladder-stile. Follow the path over three further ladder-stiles to a farm, then turn left through a small gate up past the end of a barn to a ladder-stile at the top of the slope. Continue ahead along the old field boundary, soon descending to cross a footbridge and a ladder-stile. At a cross-path at the top of the slope continue ahead alongside the fence, through a gate, past Cae-glas cottage and down its access track to a lane. Descend a path opposite to a gate, then follow the path angling down the hillside towards Ffynongower farm. Just beyond another gate bend sharp right down the farm's access track to the B4403. Follow the road left with care, facing oncoming traffic – it can be busy in summer. The road runs close to Bala Lake Railway and the shore of the lake, passing a house at Glanlyn

View over Llyn Tegid to Y Bala

Halt, then Pentrepiod halt. *The narrow gauge railway, operational since 1976, runs for 4½ miles along Llyn Tegid on the trackbed of the former Great Western Ruabon – Barmouth railway.*

5 After ⅓ mile, take a track angling back on the left, signposted to Pentre Piod Gwynant, then cross a ladder-stile on the right. Now follow the left edge of an old sunken way. At a stream by an open gateway on your right, turn left for a few yards then cross the stream and a stile. Continue up the edge of the field to pass an old gateway. About 75 yards below the field corner go half-right through a large boundary gap, across a stream and up alongside a boundary of large stones. Go through a gate, past a house and between farm outbuildings and on

down its access lane. When it bends right, keep ahead down the slope to cross a stile near a ruin. Head down the field to cross a ladder-stile onto the B4403. Cross the road, then follow it past Felindre (offering B&B). Just past the road sign for Dinas Mawdwy/ Llanuwchllyn go through a kissing gate on the right. Go down the reedy field and through a kissing gate in the bottom corner. Cross the railway line with care, then head towards the station. *(This is a permissive section by kind agreement of the Railway. Do not walk along the track.)* Go past engine sheds, through the car park to the station, where there is a cafe. Continue along the road into Llanuwchllyn. At the junction turn right through the village.

LLANUWCHLLYN TO THE SOURCE
12¾ miles

36 Llanuwchllyn to Coed Penaran and return
6¾ miles

From Llanuwchllyn, the trail continues along the Dyfrdwy Valley, crosses the infant river by stepping stones, then rises across wilder upland country above the river where it enters the forest of Coed Penaran, about 1¾ miles west of the river's source. After crossing wilder upland pasture it heads back towards Llanuwchllyn by paths and quiet lanes, with good views.

Llanuwchllyn (the church at the head of the lake) was the birthplace of two prominent Welshmen, whose statues stand at the village entrance. Regularly punished for speaking Welsh whilst at school, Sir Owen Morgan Edwards (1858–1920) later became Chief Inspector of the new Welsh Education Department established in 1907, and actively promoted Welsh learning, writing many books and magazines. His son – Sir Ifan ab Owen Edwards (1895-1970) founded the Urdd Gobaith Cymru (The Welsh League of Youth) – which blends together culture, artistic activity, outdoor pursuits and Christian piety.

1 For those coming through the northern part of Llanuwchllyn on **Route A**, after crossing the river and just beyond toilets, take a signposted path through a gate on the right. Go past two new houses to cross a stile. Now go half-right, soon with the boundary on your left to go through a gate in the corner. Head half-right across a large field, through a gate, and go up the next field to join a lane.

For those coming through Llanuwchllyn on **Route B**, take the no through road opposite Y Neuadd Bentref and follow the lane into open country.

2 When the lane splits take the right fork and follow it up to pass a bungalow, then a farm. At the next farm, go past the house and follow a waymarked path through the buildings. Continue along a green track, soon bending half-right and descending to pass between two stone barns. Follow the waymarked path through a gate and on along the green track, then head away from the fence corner to enter a small wood by a gate. Follow a path through the open woodland to join a track by Rhos Uchaf. Continue ahead along the stony track to a lane. Follow it right down to a house.

3 Here turn left and follow a track across the river and on up to cross a ladder stile on the right. Follow the course of an old track, cross a stream, and keep ahead along the field edge to cross a stile on the left into a cleared forest. Follow an old green track and after 100 yards, at a waymarker post, go half-right across rougher ground for a further 100 yards to cross a sleeper bridge and a nearby stile. Turn left and walk between the fence and the old embanked boundary to cross a stile. Keep ahead across the reedy field to a gate. Continue along the next field edge to reach a signposted path junction at a track leading to Tyn y Cefn. Continue

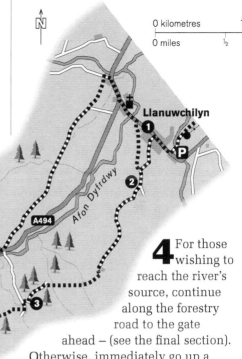

4 For those wishing to reach the river's source, continue along the forestry road to the gate ahead – (see the final section). Otherwise, immediately go up a green track on the right and through a gate. Follow the track, soon reedy and sunken, up to where a fence crosses it. A gateway in the fence corner allows you to continue up the track to a gate. Just beyond the faint reedy track splits. Keep ahead on the lower one across rough upland pasture – *with the infant river below by the forest. Nearby is an old settlement containing remains of enclosures and platform houses* – shortly joining the fence up on your right. At its end corner go through a gateway and keep ahead up the reedy field. Soon angle right to go through the facing gate in the right-hand field corner. Follow the fence on your left – *soon with a view of Llyn Tegid* – to a ladder-stile. Follow the fence-topped wall on your left beneath Moel Caws

on a higher green track alongside a low embanked boundary. When it fades keep ahead to follow the embanked boundary to a stile. Continue ahead for 30 yards to a forestry track. Turn right and follow it down to the A494. Cross the road with care, and follow it left. At a finger post, turn right down a track to a forestry road and house at Garneddwen Halt on the former Ruabon-Barmouth railway line. Go through a small gate opposite and on to cross the infant Afon Dyfrdwy by stepping stones. (If the river is in spate follow the track round to point **4**.) Go through the gate ahead, then follow the path up to the forestry road. Turn left.

Stepping stones over the infant river

down to a hidden stile in a joining fence, then down to a gateway in a wall ahead. Continue past a small ruin on your left and up the slope ahead, then follow the fence on the right to a gate. Follow the narrow green track by the fence – *with a good view of the Aran ridge* – to its corner, then continue along the track to a gate to reach the rear of a farm. Angle left to pass between the house and outbuildings, then continue along its access track.

5 After passing two barns, take the left fork towards a house and go through a gate in the right-hand corner. Go past a stone barn and along the bottom edge of two fields, then after crossing a stream, go half-right down the large field to a lane. Follow it left, past Hendre Mawr and its caravan site to the A494. Turn left past the chapel and continue up the side road. After a while the road begins a long gentle decent towards Llanuwchllyn. At a large farm complex, take a signposted path through a gate on the left. Follow the track to a stile by a bungalow onto a lane. Turn right to reach the A494. Cross the road and walk along the pavement into Llanuwchllyn, perhaps for a drink at The Eagles Inn to celebrate the end of your walking adventure. The X94 bus can be boarded from the bus stop near the PO and church to Y Bala or onward to Wrexham or Chester.

37 Coed Penaran to the source

6 miles return

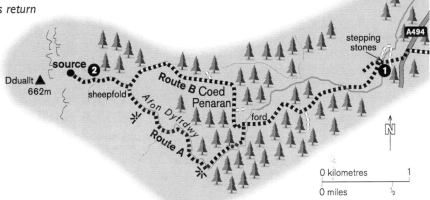

The final section of the trail continues to where the water first flows from the base of the boulder/scree covered slope of Dduallt mountain and an unexpected sight. At this remote wild spot, miles from habitation, is a tiny stone man-made building, with a large boulder forming one end. It is too small for a sheepfold and is not marked on the map. According to the outdoor writer Jim Perrin, it may once have been an ancient shrine in earlier times when springs and wells were places of special religious significance associated with healing properties.

The trail first follows a forestry road through Coed Penaran, Forestry Commission land with open access for walkers, to where it crosses the Afon Dyfrdwy. Here there are a choice of routes to the source. **Route A** is only suitable for experienced hill walkers familiar with tough upland terrain. It closely follows the infant river, little more than a wide peaty stream, through a pathless area of open forest to its perimeter, then across adjoining wild upland country, designated Open Access land, to its source. Afterwards it crosses an area of cleared forest to join the end of the forestry road (Route B), which now extends further than shown on the current OS map. This is a demanding but rewarding route across remote reedy/ tussocky/ heather terrain, with intermittent paths on the open country section, and should be avoided in poor visibility. **Route B** takes the easier approach of continuing up the extended forestry road for a further mile to its end at the edge of cleared forest less than ½ mile from the source. You then have the option of working your way across the cleared forest, rough underfoot, to join the infant river for its final short journey to the source, before returning the same way.

Please note that forestry operations will take place in stages during the next five years to remove conifers in Coed Penaran and return the land to blanket bog moorland as a habitat for black grouse and grazing by mountain ponies. The increasingly more open landscape will undoubtedly enhance the character of this section of the trail.

I After going through the gate continue up the forestry road, later crossing the Afon Dyfrdwy. When it splits keep ahead past a waymarked path/track on the left and follow the forestry road – *soon with a view of Dduallt* – up past a small quarry. Please respect the sign and do not enter the quarry, but you can continue along the road. A little further it crosses the infant river.

For **Route A** turn left and work your way along the reedy river bank through an area of cleared forest. Initially intimidating the terrain soon improves. Just after the river bends west, cross it where convenient and walk along its southern side. About 40 yards before the edge of the forest cross to the opposite bank and continue to a fence into open country. From here the Dyfrdwy heads north west alongside the forest edge towards Dduallt. Cross it and continue up its left side, later crossing a fence. At a gate in the forest perimeter fence on the right angle left across a wet reedy/tussocky area to cross the Dyfrdwy near the fence corner of a large unplanted area of forestry land. Now follow an intermittent path along the right bank of the dwindling Dyfrdwy near the fence, shortly passing a stone sheepfold [SH 821273].

2 At fence junction, pass under the wire and follow the fence left alongside the fast flowing now narrow stream towards Dduallt. Shortly leave the fence to follow the dwindling flow to its end among reeds, boulders and the mysterious man-made building beneath the imposing rocky slope of Dduallt mountain [SH 813275]. After reflecting on its possible significance and enjoying the satisfaction of having followed the Dee to its source, retrace your steps to the sheepfold. Cross the fence by a post/stone just beyond it. Go up the slope then keep ahead across the cleared forest for about 200 metres to join the end of the forestry road [SH 822275]. Follow it to a gate, after which it briefly rises before making a long steady descent past side roads to recross the Dyfrdwy. Continue down the forestry road to join the return route to Llanuwchllyn at point 4 in the previous section.

For **Route B** continue up the forestry road and at a junction keep ahead. Later when it splits go up its left fork to a good view of Dduallt, then down to a gate. Continue along the level forestry road to where it dips down to end at the edge of a large area of cleared forest [SH 822275]. The line of the Afon Dyfrdwy can be seen as it heads to its source beneath the rocky slopes of Dduallt mountain. To reach the source angle slightly left (south-west), working your way across the cleared forest towards the line of a stream running down the middle of high ground ahead for about 200 metres to overlook the Afon Dyfrdwy, now a fast flowing stream, with a stone sheepfold nearby. Descend to cross the perimeter fence to join Route A. Turn right and walk between the fence and the stream, then follow instructions in paragraph 2.

The source of the Dee

Linear walks

The good local public transport network allows each section of the trail to Llanuwchllyn to be undertaken as linear day/half-day walks of variable length, which enables people of all ages and abilities to enjoy the new walking opportunities throughout the length of the river trail at convenience and over time. Frequent buses on some sections enable local walkers or one centre visitors to undertake linear walks without a car.

Bus services can change at any time, so please check current available services and times before planning any walk. Detailed bus timetables are available from relevant local authorities and from Tourist Information Centres (See Guidance Notes and Useful Information).

I have broken the trail down into 23 linear walks, but most can be combined to make longer day walks if required. Use the buses indicated then follow the appropriate section of the Dee Way back to the starting point.

Walk 1 Hoylake to Parkgate (9¼ miles)
From Parkgate Square take the 22 or 22A bus to West Kirby station, then the Merseyrail train to Hoylake.

Walk 2 Parkgate to Burton (4 miles)
From Burton take the 22A bus to Parkgate.

Walk 3 Burton to Chester (11 miles)
From Chester bus station take the 22A bus to Burton.
*(**Walks 2 & 3** combined make a 15 mile walk from Parkgate to Chester using the 22/22A bus.)*

Walk 4 Saughall to Chester (5 miles)
From Chester bus station take 15/15A/15B to Saughall.

Walk 5 Prestatyn to Ffynnongroyw (7 miles)
From Ffynnongroyw take the 11/11A bus to Prestatyn.

Walk 6 Ffynnongroyw to Holywell (8¼ miles)
From Holywell bus station take the 11/11A bus to Ffynnongroyw.
*(**Walks 5 & 6** combined make a 15¼ mile walk from Prestatyn to Holywell.)*

Walk 7 Holywell to Flint (6¾ miles)
From the bus stop near McDonalds on the A548 in Flint (car park nearby) take the 11/11A bus to Holywell and follow the Dee Way back to Flint Castle. Go along Castle Street opposite the entrance to reach the A548 and town centre via a footbridge over the railway.

Walk 8 Flint to Connah's Quay (4½ miles)
From the main road in Connah's Quay near Dock Road take the 11/11A bus to Flint. This walk combines better with walks 7 or 9.

Walk 9 Connah's Quay to Chester (9 miles)
From Chester bus station take either the 11/11A or 10 bus to the bus stop in Connah's Quay near Dock Road. Walk along Dock Road to the quayside and on to Wepre Riverside car park.

Walk 10 Chester to Aldford (7½ miles)
From the discreet car park in Aldford [SJ 419594] walk along Church Lane to the B5130, where there is a bus stop. Take the C56 bus to Chester bus station. Head north along nearby Northgate Street to access the city walls. Go east, then follow the walls round past the cathedral to eventually descend to the Groves. Cross the Old Dee bridge and follow the river back to Aldford.

Walk 11 Aldford to Farndon (6 miles)
From Farndon riverside picnic area car park by the old bridge walk up the road to catch the C56 bus to the far end of Aldford. Go along Church Lane to the church, then follow the Dee Way back to Farndon.
*(**Walks 10 & 11** combined make a 13½ mile mainly riverside walk.)*

Walk 12 Farndon to Bangor-on-Dee (9½ or 12½ miles)
From Bangor-on-Dee (Whitchurch Road) take 146 bus to Wrexham centre to catch the C56 bus from Market Street (not main bus station) to Farndon/Holt. Follow the choice of routes back to Bangor.

Walk 13 Bangor-on-Dee to Overton (6 miles)
From Overton take the 146 bus to Bangor.

Walk 14 Overton to Chirk (7½ or 8¾ miles)
From Chirk take bus service 2 or 2A to Wrexham bus station to connect with service 146 to Overton.

Walk 15 Chirk to Froncysyllte (7¼ or 5 miles)
From Froncysyllte (small parking area by the canal off the B5434 [SJ 271413] take the 64 or 5A (Sundays) bus to Chirk. Follow **Route A** to Trevor Basin and return across Pontcysyllte aqueduct to cross a footbridge further along the canal. Alternatively follow canal **Route B** to the aqueduct, then cross under its southern end (new path) and return along the canal's other side.

Walk 16 Froncysyllte to Llangollen (5 miles)
From Market Street, Llangollen (large car park nearby) take the 64 or 5A (Sundays) bus to Froncysyllte. Access and cross the canal by a footbridge and follow the towpath across Pontcysllte aqueduct into Trevor Basin. Follow the high level Dee Way route or canal alternative back to Llangollen.
*(**Walks 15 & 16** are easily combined to make a 12¼ or 10 mile walk.)*

Walk 17 Llangollen to Glyndyfrdwy (9 miles)
Turn off the A5 at the shop in Glyndyfrdwy on the road signposted to Rhewl to find roadside parking. Return to the A5, turn left to a bus stop by a butcher's shop. Take the X94 bus to Llangollen. Now follow the Dee Way back to cross the bridge over the river at Glyndyfrdwy. Go past the railway station back to the start. An alternative is to park near the station and take the Llangollen steam railway to Llangollen.

Walk 18 Glyndyfrdwy to Corwen (7¼ miles)
From Corwen take the X94 bus to Glyndyfrdwy, alighting near the shop. Go down the road signposted to Rhewl through the village, past the station to cross the bridge over the river. The train from Carrog to Glyndyfrdwy offers an alternative 4 mile walk.
(The 15½ mile section of the Dee Way from Llangollen to Corwen can easily be undertaken utilising the X94 bus from Corwen.)

Walk 19 Corwen to Cynwyd (6 miles)
From the centre of Cynwyd (off-road parking at SJ 057412) take the X94 bus to Corwen.

Walk 20 Cynwyd to Llandrillo (4 or 7 miles)
From the Dudley Arms in Llandrillo (nearby riverside car park) take the X94
bus to Cynwyd, and follow the choice of routes back.
(Walks 19 & 20 are easily combined to make a 10 or 13 mile walk.)

Walk 21 Llandrillo to Llandderfel (4¾ miles)
From Llandderfel (car parking by stream opposite 19th National school) take
the X94 bus to Llandrillo.

Walk 22 Llandderfel to Y Bala (4½ miles)
 From the High Street in Y Bala, take the X 94 bus to Llandderfel.
(Walks 21 & 22 are easily combined to make a 9¼ mile walk.)

Walk 23 Y Bala to Llanuwchllyn (8¼ or 7 miles)
For **Route A**, take the X94 bus from near the PO and church in Llanuwchllyn
to Y Bala. For **Route B** take the X94 bus by Station Road at the southern end
of Llanuwchllyn to Y Bala (SNP car park by bridge). Follow the relevant route
back to Llanuwchllyn. The Bala Lake Railway (4 trains daily in season) also
provides an opportunity to combine a scenic lakeside railway ride with a
shorter **Route B**.

Dee Estuary Walk

Combining both the Welsh and English routes from Prestatyn and Hoylake
respectively to Chester, once the head of the estuary and an important port
since Roman times, makes a fascinating all-year round 57½ mile walk. The
estuary offers diverse coastal scenery including beaches, sand-dunes, low
cliffs, saltmarshes and mudflats, as well as a little known section of tidal river
to the heart of old Chester.

The estuary constantly changes in character with the ebb and flow of the
fast changing tide, and offers extensive views across to either the Wirral
peninsula or the Welsh Hills. Enjoy watching the large number of seabirds and waders (binoculars recommended) and learn about the estuary's
maritime and industrial history, including the fluctuating fortunes of its
various small ports on both sides of the river during the many centuries that
the Dee was an important shipping route.

The full estuary walk can be undertaken in either direction. It can also be undertaken as short linear walks using local bus services. This is a particularly valuable option in winter when days are short, but the estuary is alive with thousands of overwintering birds.

As the Dee is a RAMSAR site of international importance for nature conservation, please pass through sensitive areas at high tide quickly and quietly to avoid disturbance to roosting birds.

Llyn Tegid Walk

Routes A & B of the Dee Way between Y Bala and Llanuwchllyn combine to make a superb 14 mile upland circuit of Llyn Tegid, offering panoramic views of the lake and surrounding hills and mountains. At Llanuwchllyn refreshments are available at the Eagles inn, and Bala Lake Railway station cafe in season.

Start: Car park at eastern end of Llyn Tegid [SH 928354] or the Snowdonia National Park Lakeside car park [SH 921355]. From the second sentence in section **2** follow **Route A** from the car park to the alternative lakeside car park and the A494. Continue with **Route A** to Llanuwchllyn.

Continue through the village, then near its far end go along Station Road to Bala Lake Railway station. Go through the car park, past the engine sheds and alongside the line. *(This is a permissive section by kind agreement of the Railway. Do not walk along the track.)* About 100 yards beyond the last shed cross the line to a kissing gate and go up the reedy field to the road. Follow it past Felindre, then cross a ladder-stile on the right. Go half-left up two fields, then follow an access lane up to a farm. Go between outbuildings, past the house and through a gate beyond. Follow the boundary on your left down to cross a stream. Bear left down the long field edge to cross a stile and a stream, then follow the edge of a sunken way to a ladder-stile and a lane (point 5 on the map).

Continue with care along the nearby B4403 past Pentrepiod halt and a house close by the railway. Shortly, turn up the access track to Ffynongower. At the house, bend sharp left up through a gate and on up to a lane. Go through the gate opposite and follow the track up to pass Cae-glas (gates), then go along the field edge to cross a ladder-stile/footbridge in a narrow dingle. Follow an old field boundary to a ladder-stile. Go down towards a farm to pass to the right of outbuildings. After a small gate, cross the nearby

Bala Lake Railway

ladder-stile, then follow the path over three further ladder-stiles to reach a stony track. Follow it down and just before a bridge over the river, follow a path to cross a footbridge just upstream (point **4**).

Follow the nearby road along the valley, then take a signposted path along a track on the right past farm buildings. Later follow the path behind a house and through a gate beyond. Follow the waymarked path through a large then small gate. At the fence corner, keep ahead, soon rejoining it. After a further 50 yards, the waymarked path descends alongside a stream. After about 200 yards, as the slope levels out turn right across the stream and on to cross a ladder-stile/stream/ladder-stile. The path continues alongside the fence, then angles up the bracken-covered hillside to eventually reach a ladder-stile at a great viewpoint (point 3).

Join a track just beyond and follow it down to cross a ladder-stile, then descend to a road. Follow the signposted path across the open hillside towards Y Bala, later descending and meandering down to a stile. The path continues down to a stream near a cottage, then up to a fence corner. Continue alongside the fence, then go past a wood corner and down a field past a house to a stile in the corner. The path descends to a driveway which you follow up to nearby Bala Lake Hotel. Pass behind the main building, through the rear car park and continue along a track past farm buildings. Shortly, cross a stile on the left, and go down two fields, then across a footbridge over Bala Lake Railway and on to the B4403. Cross the old bridge opposite, go along the B4391 and follow the pavement along the end of the lake, where seats make a fitting final stop to enjoy the views along the lake.

Llangollen railway station, with Castell Dinas Bran beyond

Guidance Notes & Useful Information

General advice

In this guidebook I have divided the Dee Way into 37 short sections containing the detailed route descriptions, accompanying maps, and notes on local history etc.

Accommodation along the trail, whilst variable in quantity, does allow some flexibility in planning for those wishing to undertake the trail as a continuous walk of 10 – 14 days. It is recommended though that accommodation, especially where limited, is booked in advance. There are many places of interest along the route so please build time into your itinerary to visit and enjoy them. A suggested itinerary is:

Hoylake – Parkgate – Chester or Prestatyn – Holywell – Chester

Chester – Farndon – Bangor-on-Dee – Chirk – Llangollen – Corwen – Llandrillo – Y Bala/Llanuwchllyn

From Y Bala, there are choices dependent on whether you are intending to complete the tougher final section to the source, which has to be combined with the penultimate section from and to Llanuwchllyn. As there is plenty of accommodation in Y Bala, one option is to stay there for more than one night, leaving overnight gear etc, and completing the remainder of the trail combined with the X94 bus, possibly including the circuit of Llyn Tegid in your itinerary.

Although undertaking sections of the trail as day walks can be undertaken throughout the year, for those planning to walk the whole trail continuously, the timing from Spring to early Autumn is a personal choice. Perhaps my preferred season for a river walk is Spring/early Summer when nature stirs. But the long balmy days of summer and the changing colours of autumn offer their own appeal. It is as well to remember though that the river is prone to flooding, especially in the borderland flood plain after heavy rain, and as we have seen in recent years, this can occur at anytime during the year.

Good walking boots are required, along with appropriate clothing to protect against the elements. Be prepared for any weather, which can vary from spring snow to hot sunshine during the summer. The weather generally changes more rapidly in the hills and mountains than the coast and borderlands, with rain and mist descending quickly. But do not forget the suntan cream – all day walking in the sun while unprotected can cause discomfort and be harmful. Carry plenty of drink and food, especially on those sections where facilities are limited, and emergency equipment, including a small torch, which will also be useful when passing through the canal tunnel near Chirk.

For the long distance walker it is possible to complete the route from a limited number of accommodation bases, by a combination of car and bus in both directions or, with careful planning, by bus alone. I have successfully used the combination of car and bus from one or two campsite bases to complete several long distance walks in this way, carrying only a day bag.

Note that the riverside section past the Roodee in Chester is closed on race days, so enquire in advance, or take the city walls alternative route.

Whilst walking along the Dee estuary please remember that it is a RAMSAR site (named after the town of Ramsar in Iran) of international importance for its birds and nature conservation, so try to avoid any disturbance to roosting birds.

The route follows public Rights of Way or permissive paths, while the final section to the source crosses designated Open Access land. Visit the Countryside Council for Wales web site (www.ccw.gov.uk) in advance to check on any temporary closures that may apply.

Please remember that changes in details on the ground – ie. new stiles and gates, field boundaries, path diversions etc can occur at any time. Individual local authorities may upgrade and waymark sections for local promoted routes. Also remember that the condition of paths can vary according to season and weather. If you encounter any problems please report these to the relevant bodies listed below:

Flintshire County Council RoW 01352 701233/4
Flintshire Coastal Unit 01244 814931
Wirral Country Park 0151 648 4371/3884 for the Wirral Way
Cheshire County Council RoW 01606 971825
Wrexham County Borough RoW 01978 292057
Shropshire County Council RoW 01743 251000
Denbighshire County Council RoW 01824 706872
Gwynedd Council RoW 01341 422341

There may be future improvements to The Dee Way route, especially in Flintshire, where it is hoped that the Council will realise its long term plan to extend the new off-road Dee Coastal Path further along the estuary edge from Connah's Quay to Flint, so removing a currently unavoidable section of roadside walking.

Maps

The route is covered by the following Ordnance Survey maps:

Landranger 1:50000: 116/108/117/126/125

Explorer 1:25000: 266 Wirral & Chester; 265 Clwydian Range; 257 Crewe & Nantwich; 256 Wrexham & Llangollen; 255 Llangollen & Berwyn; **Outdoor Leisure** 18 Harlech & Bala; Outdoor Leisure 23 Cadair Idris & Bala Lake.

Facilities

The trail passes through various towns and villages that offer a variable range of services. For long distance walkers the main considerations are overnight accommodation, evening meal options and refreshment stops/shops on the route. The internet is now a good source of information for planning your walk. The following information is a guide, but details may change. Sadly, in the current economic climate, village shops and pubs are under threat of closure. If you are planning to call at a pub en route I suggest you contact it in advance to check its opening times and whether it serves food.

Hoylake to Chester

Hoylake and West Kirby offer a range of facilities. Thurstaston Visitor Centre, open all year, provides drinks. Parkgate has restaurants, stores, take-aways, inns, a PO/Shop and limited B&B accommodation. There may be additional accommodation in nearby Neston. The route passes an inn at Little Neston, a PO in Burton, with a coffee shop at nearby Burton Manor. Saughall has a PO/stores and pub, while Chester offers a comprehensive range of facilities.

Prestatyn to Holywell

Prestatyn offers a range of facilities. Talacre has an inn and small shops, including a baker's. Ffynnongroyw has limited accommodation, inns, a PO/shop, and take-away. There is Mostyn Lodge Hotel on the A548, an inn at Mostyn and three at Llannerch-y-mor, plus a café at Abakhan. Greenfield has shops and inns and a take-away. Holywell has B&Bs and a range of facilities.

Holywell to Chester

Bagillt has shops and inns. Flint has a range of facilities, but no registered B&B accommodation. However, there are two farm guesthouses just off the route at Oakenholt. The route passes a riverside inn at Connah's Quay and one near the Blue Bridge, and there are shops etc in Connah's Quay and Queensferry. There is a motel at Garden City. There are no facilities between Queensferry and Chester.

Chester to Farndon

Aldford has a PO/shop and an inn just off the route. Farndon has B&Bs, inns, stores, chemists, PO, and meal options. Nearby Holt has a general store, an award-winning butcher's shop, and inns.

Farndon to Bangor-on-Dee

On Route A, there are no facilities between Holt and Bangor. On Route B there is an inn in both Shocklach and Worthenbury. Bangor-on-Dee has B&Bs, inns offering meals, and two shops/PO. There is a campsite at the racecourse 1 mile outside the village.

Bangor-on-Dee to Chirk

There is an inn at Overton Bridge serving meals. Overton has a Post Office, shop, chemists, an inn providing meals, and a B&B outside the village. Chirk has B&Bs, shops, eating options, inns, a chemist, community hospital, PO and banking facilities.

Chirk to Llangollen

Ty Mawr Country Park's small shop offers cold drinks etc. On the canalside route, nearby Ffroncysyllte has an inn and shop. Trevor and Ffroncysyllte have B&B. There is an inn at Trevor Basin and one mid-way on the canal route to Llangollen. There are a range of facilities at Llangollen.

Llangollen to Corwen

The route passes an inn at Rhewl. At Glyndyfrdwy there is a tea-room at the station, open during high season, and a shop on the A5. Carrog has an inn, PO/shop, campsite, with a tearoom at nearby Carrog Station. Corwen has B&Bs and other facilities.

Corwen to Llandrillo

Cynwyd has inns serving food (*at lunchtimes on selected days only*), a post office/shop that reportedly can make good sandwishes to order, a fish & chip shop and limited B&B accommodation. Llandrillo has two B&B's, an inn (*not open every day*), restaurant (*open at weekends*) and a shop.

Llandrillo to Y Bala

Llandderfel has a PO/shop. There is bunkhouse accommodation at Tomen-y-castell (01678 520738) on the route and a B&B at Llanfor. Y Bala has B&Bs and a range of facilities.

Y Bala to Llanuwchllyn

Llanuwchyllyn has one B&B near the school and another just off the B4403, 1 mile from the village (Felindre, 01678 540389) passed on Route B, a camp site by the station, an inn serving food, and a PO/shop. There is a café at Bala Lake Railway station at Llanuwchllyn (*open daily July/August, but not Mondays & Fridays other months* – 01678 540666).

There are no facilities on the final route section.

Tourist Information Centres

The following offer information and an accommodation booking service.

Wirral/Cheshire: Birkenhead (0151 691 8342; www. wirral.gov.uk); Chester (01244 351609 /402385; www.chestertourism.com)
North East Wales: Rhyl (01745 344515; www.rhyl-prestatyn.co.uk);
Prestatyn (01745 889092); Mold (01352 759331), Wrexham (01978 292015),
Llangollen (01978 860828); www.borderlands.co.uk covers the last three.
Gwynedd: Y Bala (01678 521021)

Transport

Both Prestatyn and Hoylake are easily accessible via the National Rail network from any part of the UK. Ending the trail at Llanuwchllyn, provides access to the regular X94 bus service from Barmouth to Wrexham or Chester, from where there is a connection to both the National Railway and National Express networks.

Unlike many long distance trails, the Dee Way is supported by easily accessible public transport throughout its length. The local bus services which I used to research the route were reliable, clean and comfortable. They offer good views of the countryside and communities they pass through, and are an enjoyable part of the visiting experience.

The Wirral link to Chester

No. **22** bus provides an hourly Mon – Sat service between Chester and West Kirby station, calling at Parkgate and Hewall. No. **22A** operates twice daily via Burton From the station there are frequent (*four an hour*) Merseyrail trains to Hoylake.

There are frequent buses (**15/15A/15B**) between Saughall and Chester (*Mon-Sat*), *hourly Sunday.*

The North Wales coast link to Chester

The Dee Corridor Route from Prestatyn to Chester is particularly well served by the Arriva Cymru **11/11A** bus service (*half-hourly Mon – Sat ; two hourly*

Sundays) Services **10** and **12** also run regularly between Connah's Quay – Chester. There are also regular train services between Chester and Prestatyn, calling at Flint and Shotton.

The Borderlands between Chester and Chirk

Bus services through this more sparsely populated area are more limited, but quite reasonable. These include Huxley Coaches service **C56** Chester – Wrexham, calling at Aldford, Churton, Farndon and Holt (*hourly Mon – Sat*); GHA Coaches service **146** Whitchurch – Wrexham, calling at Overton and Bangor-on-Dee (*hourly Mon – Sat, limited Sunday service*), and Arriva Cymru services **2/2A** Chirk – Wrexham (*half-hourly Mon – Sat*)

The Dee Valley to Llanuwchllyn

This section is very well served by Arriva Cymru X94 Chester-Wrexham-Barmouth bus (*a regular Mon – Sat, and limited Sunday service*), initially along the historic A5 Dee corridor, linking key local communities between Llangollen and Llanuwchllyn. Other useful services are the **64** and the **5A** between Chirk – Llangollen
Llangollen Railway also runs services between Llangollen and Carrog [Talking timetable 01978 860951] Bala Lake Railway operates a narrow gauge service along Llyn Tegid to Llanuwchllyn [01678 540666].

Please note that bus services are subject to amendment, so always check current timetables.

Public Transport Enquiries

Traveline 0871 200 2233

National Rail 08457 484950
National Express 08705 808080.

Cheshire Bus Line 0845 140 2666 www.cheshire.gov.uk/transport
Merseytravel 0151 236 7676 www.merseytravel.gov.uk
Flintshire Busline 01352 704035 www.flintshire.gov.uk
Wrexham Bus Line 01978 266166 or www.wrexham.gov.uk
Denbighshire Bus Line 01824 706968 www.denbighshire.gov.uk/transport
Bws Gwynedd 01286 679535 www.gwynedd.gov.uk

Updates to the route

It is inevitable that on a long-distance route such as The Dee Way details will change over time. You can help fellow walkers by letting us know of any modifications to the route, which we can initially publish on the web site and then incorporate into future editions.
Please email any such information to:
kittiwake@btconnect.com
or you can write to:
The Dee Way, **Kittiwake**
3 Glantwymyn Village Workshops, Glantwymyn, Machynlleth SY20 8LY

View any changes which have been notified to us at:
www.thedeeway.com

Your photos

If you would like to share your photos of The Dee Way with other walkers please email your jpegs to kittiwake@btconnect.com and we will consider them for inclusion on the web site. *We can not offer any payment for their use, or accept transparencies or prints, but all photos will be credited.*

Please always follow the Countryside Code

Be safe – plan ahead and follow any signs
Leave gates and property as you find them
Protect plants and animals, and take your litter home
Keep dogs under close control
Consider other people

Other Kittiwake Guides by David Berry

Available at local bookshops and Tourist Information Centres,
or online at: www.kittiwake-books.com
See detailed descriptions at www.davidberrywalks.co.uk

Walks on the **Clwydian Range** – 22 walks

More Walks on the **Clwydian Range** – 23 walks

Walks in the **Vale of Clwyd** – 22 walks

Walks around **Llangollen & the Dee Valley** – 20 walks

Walks around **Holywell & Halkyn Mountain** – 20 walks

Walks in the **Hidden Heart of North Wales** – 21 walks

Walks around the **Berwyn Mountains & the Ceiriog Valley** – 32 walks

Walks around **Betws-y-Coed & the Conwy Valley** – 24 walks

Walks in the **Heart of Snowdonia** – 36 walks

Walks on the **Llŷn Peninsula** – 28 walks

Walks around **Y Bala & Penllyn** – 20 walks

Walks around **Barmouth & the Mawddach Estuary** – 20 walks

Walks around **Anglesey (Ynys Môn)** – 40 walks

Walks around **Conwy** – 30 walks

Walks around **Ruabon Mountain** – 28 walks

Walks around **Llandudno** – 30 walks

Walks around **Penmachno & Ysbyty Ifan** – 24 walks

KITTIWAKE

Walks guides which detail superb routes
in most parts of Wales.

From Anglesey and Llandudno to the Brecon Beacons,
and from Machynlleth and Welshpool to Pembrokeshire and the Llŷn,
they offer a range of carefully researched routes
with something for all abilities.

Each guide has been compiled and written by a
dedicated author who really knows their particular area.

They are all presented in the **KITTIWAKE** clear
and easy-to-use style

For latest details of the expanding range, visit:

www.kittiwake-books.com

KITTIWAKE
3 Glantwymyn Village Workshops
Glantwymyn, Machynlleth
Montgomeryshire SY20 8LY